Starting Out in the Thirties

ALFRED KAZIN

STARTING OUT IN THE THIRTIES

Cornell University Press

ITHACA AND LONDON

Cornell Paperbacks edition first published 1989
by Cornell University Press.

The author wishes to thank the *Atlantic Monthly* for permission
to reprint material which first appeared in its pages.

The lines from STUDS LONIGAN by James T. Farrell are
reprinted by permission of the publisher, The Vanguard Press,
copyright 1932, 1934, 1935, © 1960, 1962, 1963, by James T. Farrell.

Library of Congress Cataloging-in-Publication Data

Kazin, Alfred, 1915–
  Starting out in the thirties / Alfred Kazin.
    p. cm.
  Reprint. Originally published: Boston : Little, Brown, 1965.
  ISBN 0-8014-9562-8 (alk. paper)
    1. Kazin, Alfred, 1915–   . 2. Critics—United States—Biography.
I. Title.
PS29.K38A3 1989
809—dc19
[B]
                                              88-31709
                                              CIP

PRINTED IN THE UNITED STATES OF AMERICA

*The paper in this book is acid-free and meets the guidelines
for permanence and durability of the Committee
on Production Guidelines for Book Longevity of the
Council on Library Resources.*

FOR ANN AND CATHRAEL

RALPH: Mom, I love this girl. . . .

BESSIE: So go knock your head against the wall. . . . If she dropped in the ocean I don't lift a finger. . . . With me it's one thing — a boy should have respect for his own future.

CLIFFORD ODETS, *Awake and Sing* (1935)

CONTENTS

PART ONE 1934

supernatural event which one might await with perfect faith, but which had no immediate relevance to my life. "Socialism" was a way of life, since everyone else I knew in New York was a Socialist, more or less; but I was remarkably detached from it intellectually, and spent my days reading Blake and Lawrence and Whitman. I felt moral compulsions to be a Socialist, since the society in which sixteen million people were jobless that summer and a million on strike did not seem to admit saving except by a Socialist government. But my social-ism, though I felt it deeply, did not require any conscious personal assent or decision on my part; I was a Socialist as so many Americans were "Christians"; I had always lived in a Socialist atmosphere. But if anyone who had thought his own way into socialism had questioned me sharply as to what I accepted or did not accept of Marxism, he would have discov-ered very little to please him except my violent class prejudice. I was a literary radical, indifferent to economics, suspicious of organization, planning, Marxist solemnity and intellectual system-building; it was the rebels of literature, the great wres-tlers-with-God, Thor with his mighty hammer, the poets of unlimited spiritual freedom, whom I loved — Blake, Emer-son, Whitman, Nietzsche, Lawrence. I had watched Com-munists break up Socialist meetings and in February I had seen them throwing chairs from the balconies of Madison Square Garden down on the decent trade unionists who had met to honor the Socialists of Vienna hanged by Dollfuss; for three years I had had the law on every possible subject handed down to me by classmates who were interested less in the Revolution than in demonstrating their intellectual grasp of everything at once, and just then I was sick of Communists. I had the deepest contempt for those middle-class and doctrinaire radicals who, after graduating from Harvard or Yale in the Twenties, had made it a matter of personal honor to become Marxists, and who now worried in the *New Masses* whether Proust should be read after the Revolution and why there seemed to be no simple proletarians in the novels of André Malraux.

I felt myself to be a radical, not an ideologue; I was proud of the revolutionary yet wholly literary tradition in American writing to which I knew that I belonged, and would say over to myself, from *Axel's Castle*, the last, woven sentence of Edmund Wilson's chapter on Proust: "Proust is perhaps the last great historian of the loves, the society, the intelligence, the diplomacy, the literature and the art of the Heartbreak House of capitalist culture; and the little man with the sad appealing voice, the metaphysician's mind, the Saracen's beak, the ill-fitting dress-shirt and the great eyes that seem to see all about him like the many-faceted eyes of a fly, dominates the scene and plays host in the mansion where he is not long to be master." I lived in the Heartbreak House of capitalist culture, waiting for it to stand accused by all writers worthy of the name. I looked to literature for strong social argument, intellectual power, human liberation. If anyone had bothered to point out the inconsistencies in my intellectual affections, I would not have been ashamed. Salvation would come by the word, the long-awaited and fatefully exact word that only the true writer would speak. After three years of City College in the depths of the depression — engulfed by Socialists who were Norman Thomas Socialists, old-line Social Democrats, Austro-Marxists; Communists who were Stalinist centrists, Trotskyite leftists, Lovestoneite right-wingers, Musteites and Fieldites; Zionists who were Progressive Labor Zionists, left Socialist Zionists and Religious Zionists — all the most accomplished philosophers ever born to the New York streets, tireless virtuosi who threw radical argument at each other morning, noon and night with the same curves and smashes with which they played ping-pong at each other in the college basement that smelled of the oily sandwiches that we brought from home — I was not worshipful of ideologists. Yet I believed in socialism, if not in the savage "proletarian" exclusiveness of the Communists at this time — before the growing power of Hitler and the Spanish Civil War induced a united front. I thought of socialism simply as a moral idea, an invocation of History in all its righteous sweep. At the moment this sweep, this eventual deliverance of mankind from material hardship, seemed very far from the realities of my life. A bleak New York summer was before me, I had no job and simply no idea what to do with myself.

It was the militant, too knowing sociological emphasis of the *Times* review that aroused me. The reviewer was John Chamberlain, who had become important to many of us for the brilliance and liveliness with which he had inaugurated a daily literary column in the staid old *Times.* Chamberlain had been reporting a recent book on America's youth by a professional youth leader who had been a Fascist and was presently (I guessed this from the review) a Communist. I knew all about professional youth leaders; the city college saw many of them, four and five years after graduation, still holding forth at street corners just outside the college walls. Youth leaders never seemed to graduate out of the class of youth. There was one of them, expelled from college because he had led a physical attack on Italian students, supposedly all Fascists, touring American colleges, whom one could see any day of the week, either at City College or Columbia — he was literally a professional agitator — working on a circle of students with a look of detached and professional hauteur. His personal arrogance had always infuriated me; he was always on podiums, street-corner platforms, in front of the statue of Alma Mater at Columbia, looking *down.* And it was this arrogance and knowingness, which had oozed out of the professional youth leader into the

review by John Chamberlain, whom I usually admired, that woke me from my torpor that hot afternoon in the subway. I hated all abstract talk of youth and the problems of youth; *I* was youth, afraid to go home without a job. Chamberlain's programmatic remarks seemed to me condescending, his manner unfeeling; I was convinced that he knew nothing about the subject; even his bothering to review such a book showed a highly abstract mind. *I* was youth — out of college for the year, useless, driven as an alley cat. What the hell does this fellow know about it anyway?

On a sudden impulse I got off at Times Square and made my way up to the *Times* — and to my utter astonishment found Chamberlain in and perfectly willing to hear me out. Chamberlain was just over thirty then, but he looked twenty, and was so boyish and unpretentious in his manner that all my anger at his inhuman "progressivism" quickly vanished in the glow of that afternoon's talk. To be able to talk to him was so unexpected that I tumbled over in my excitement, went deliriously from subject to subject, but always returned the talk to "youth" for fear that he might think I had exhausted my reason for coming. Chamberlain astounded me; in those days, he astounded everyone. He looked young, ingenuous, carelessly one of the boys, with his tousled blond hair and his torn white shirt; he made radicalism seem as American as baseball. It was not until I got to know him better that I realized how abstract his mind was — before the decade's flames were out, Chamberlain's reaction against Communism was to make him an apologist for the American businessman; with him one cause led to another. He lived on ideas, "notions" of things, so completely missing the color and emotion of the human crisis behind them that it was possible to talk to him about anything, to talk to him all the time, without his entertaining the slightest curiosity about the human beings we discussed.

Chamberlain was the golden boy of a generation of ideologues; he was surrounded by radical intellectuals, he had even published a radical critique of the progressive movement called *Farewell to Reform*, "Being a History of the Rise, Life and Decay of the Progressive Mind in America," which ended with the declaration: "However we look at it, eventual constriction stares us in the face. And that is why a contemplation of 'reform' . . . is productive of no further hopes in its tenets. The situation, looked upon with intelligence and considered as a long-range proposition, can lead to but one of two personal conclusions: it can make one either a cynic or a revolutionist." Chamberlain looked like Charles Augustus Lindbergh shyly starting out alone for Paris, like Gary Cooper at the end of a western modestly warding off a kiss. He was lean, handsome, kindly and awkward — while his conversation was all Veblen, Marx, Pareto, Beard, Sorokin, Spengler and William Graham Sumner. He never seemed to tire of turning over "ideas," for like many another middle-class American who had learned to resent capitalist society, he was looking hard for alternatives. His father was a wholesale furniture dealer in New Haven. The Chamberlains had been battered by the depression. His unprecedented and much-admired success as the "radical" first daily book critic of the *Times* — in no period but the early Thirties could Chamberlain's reviews have been a daily feature of the *Times* — was due to a stimulating, unorthodox, generous interest in ideas that made people grateful for his good faith in considering every social idea without lending himself abjectly to any one. Intellectuals in the subway would open the *Times* first to Chamberlain's book column; our unrest had reached as far as Forty-third Street. Chamberlain even looked like a Yale man's idea of a Yale man, and except for his careless clothes, like his classmates on Madison Avenue who spent their days thinking up slogans designed to make you buy toothpaste, soap and deodorants. His casualness impressed me deeply. Though he looked the all-American amateur in the company of highbrows whose opinions he respectfully listened to as he browsed through the social ideologies, Chamberlain, while always firmly rejecting Marxism as a panacea, associated himself with the radical cause as much as any writer did in the accelerating crisis that led full smash into the Nazi-Soviet pact and the outbreak of war. He seemed perpetually in search of new ideas and had become an intellectual journalist, a type as peculiar to the Thirties as Mencken had been to the Twenties; he personified to himself the crisis of the American middle class, of the old bourgeois certainties. The chilling deliberateness with which John Chamberlain was able to consider the formation of a radical party interested in more than reform, the possibilities of taking power, the confiscation of inherited wealth, all demonstrated the bankruptcy of normal middle-class standards, the crisis of middle-class Americans from small towns, of Yale graduates. The new style was Chamberlain's rambling flirtation with radical ideas, a willingness to consider *anything*, so long as it kept alive the possibility of creating a new society.

Chamberlain was interested in me that afternoon because I seemed to have an idea; at least I talked about ideas. As I was to learn later, one could never talk to Chamberlain about imaginative literature, music, painting, women; he never talked anything but social ideas. He was so absorbed in our talk that he still had his daily piece to finish, and when it became urgent for him to send his copy down, I watched with awe as he banged out his review for the day, rattling over the keys like a man who never had to stop for a moment. When the thing was done and he had sent it off, he eagerly leaned back in his chair to finish the point about Veblen that he had been making. It was only when evening came on and he realized that it was time for him to go home that it occurred to me to ask him for some help in getting a job. He looked at me with a puzzled frown when I showed him my college essays on Henry Vaughan and John Donne, laughed, and then sent me down to the *New Republic* with a scribbled recommendation — "here's an intelligent radical" — that I be given a chance to review.

So, thanks to Chamberlain, I was given the push I needed, and that hot and miserable summer I had dreaded so much I managed to earn a little writing book reviews for the *New Republic, Scribner's,* and the Sunday papers. To my surprise — I had never thought of criticism as an occupation — I suddenly found a way of writing, a form, a path to the outside world. The *New Republic* was not merely a publication but a cause and the center of many causes. I had a chance to meet writers in a society which in 1934 was still not far removed from the old Bohemia of Greenwich Village and Chelsea. The *New Republic* was still in its original brownstone in Chelsea, far west on Twenty-first Street near the piers, across from the General Theological Seminary — a backwater street which now, lined with brownstones and wearing that cracked, dusty, shabby air of old New York rooming houses and decayed storefronts, looks as if it had been painted by Edward Hopper and had once set the stage for Van Wyck Brooks's 1918 essay *Letters and Leadership:* ". . . a certain spot in New York where I often ruminate in the summer noontime, a lovely, sunny, windy plaza surrounded by ramshackle hoardings and warehouses unfinished and already half in ruin." In 1934 the *New Republic* looked distinguished to me in its consciously democratic patrician-intellectual way; when you entered the front doorway at 421 West Twenty-first, you saw the editors and the editorial secretaries bounding up and down the stairway, and in the narrow Victorian rooms the clatter of typewriters and the

Germany, the Germany of those Socialists who put out political pamphlets with throbbing red arrows on the covers showing
Hitler's designs against Poland, Russia, France. But the age of
Hitler was in full swing. Hitler and Mussolini had met at
Venice in June. And now Mussolini's little man Dollfuss, having fulfilled the boss's orders to destroy Austrian socialism,
was in his turn ambushed by the Austrian Nazis and bled to
death on the beautifully polished floors of the Chancellery in
Vienna. That summer, Hindenburg died and Hitler took Germany over completely as "Premier-President." That summer,
Upton Sinclair won the Democratic primary nomination for
governor in California on the "EPIC" program — End Poverty
In California. That summer, the drought got worse and more
and more Okies crawled out of the Dust Bowl in their jalopies.

Trouble was in the air every day now, and whatever else
you could say of them, the "new" writers looked as if they
had been born to trouble — as in fact they had been, for
they were usually the products of city streets, factories and
farms. More than the age of the ideologue, of the literary revolutionary and the "proletarian" novelist, roles usually created
within the Communist movement, the Thirties in literature
were the age of the plebes — of writers from the working
class, the lower class, the immigrant class, the non-literate
class, from Western farms and mills — those whose struggle
was to survive. When you thought of the typical writers of the
Twenties, you thought of rebels from "good" families — Dos
Passos, Hemingway, Fitzgerald, Cummings, Wilson, Cowley.
What was new about the writers of the Thirties was not so
much their angry militancy, which many shared, as their background; writers now came from anywhere. So many of the
writers who seemed to me, when I was twenty, really to *be*
writers wore a proletarian scowl on their faces as familiar as
the cigarette butt pasted in their mouths. There was a proud

and conscious sense of personal "vitality," a flourish of dangerous experiences, that I saw in the sharp faces of James T. Farrell and Robert Cantwell, of Clifford Odets and Elia Kazan. It was a time of such endless storm, of such turbulence every day of social crisis, that the drama of the depression and of Hitler's coming to power was immediately documented for me in the savage unleashed hope with which the banked-up experience of the plebes, of Jews, Irishmen, Negroes, Armenians, Italians, was coming into American books. The real excitement of the new period was in the explosion of personal liberation which such writers brought in from the slums, farms and factories. Robert Cantwell had worked in a plywood factory in the far West, learning the craft of the novel from Henry James and imposing a highly literary symbolism on the factory system. James T. Farrell had worked as a clerk in an express company and in a cigar store. Edward Dahlberg's mother had run a barbershop in Kansas City and he had been a hobo before trying his luck at college. Albert Halper had worked in a mail-order house in Chicago. Daniel Fuchs came from one Brooklyn slum, Williamsburg, and Henry Roth from another, Brownsville; Richard Wright from a tenant farm in Mississippi; John Steinbeck had worked on farms and in a sugar refinery, and had laid bricks for the new Madison Square Garden; Erskine Caldwell, though his father was a Presbyterian minister, had worked as a mill laborer, farm hand and waiter; Nelson Algren had tended a filling station in Texas and Henry Miller had worked up and down New York before driving himself wild as a personnel boss at Western Union. With ideology or without ideology, they were typical of the new writers who came up in the Thirties, and they understandably flourished their experience, their hard knocks, their life on the road, their days on the picket line and in the hiring hall.

In the Thirties the world suddenly seemed open to writers

who had nothing to go back to, writers who often were dizzy and grandiloquent, like the young William Saroyan, because they knew that there was no tradition to hold them down, and for whom writing was, literally, a way of saving one's life. Saroyan's famous rhapsody-before-death in *Story* magazine, "The Daring Young Man on the Flying Trapeze," expressed perfectly the clownishness of the young writer too conscious of being a nobody, a greaseball, an outlander, but who delivered himself every time he sat down to the typewriter. The story was gay with the delirium of a young man's oncoming death from starvation; starvation expressed perfectly the sense of the outer world in 1934 as implacable, ungiving; empty air on which a young man felt the possible exuberance of death as he went up and down the city streets, up and down, in a hunger float surrounded by nothing. "I took to writing at an early age," Saroyan was to write many years later, "to escape from meaninglessness, uselessness, unimportance, insignificance, poverty, enslavement, ill health, despair, madness, and all manner of other unattractive, natural, and inevitable things."

This was the real feeling behind the new realists of the Thirties. There were old-school editors like J. Donald Adams, directing the *New York Times Book Review*, who admired certain genteel novelists so much that he could approve of no deviation from the limply lyrical tone that they had made his norm for the American novel; Adams tried still to "uphold standards." There was not a Sunday that he did not publish, by one of the triple-named New England deaconesses who regularly reviewed fiction for him, some resounding attack on the immorality of current American fiction and the shocking deterioration of literary standards since the death of Edith Wharton. But J. Donald Adams, with his further fondness for printing White Russian émigrés in the *Book Review*, was necessary to our sense of "militancy," to our radicalism; he defined the opposition. He made all these roughs out of the slums of Chicago and Brooklyn feel that they were in the great unpopular tradition of modern literature, with Joyce and Eliot. Old newspapermen like Adams, and gentlemanly literary editors out of the academy like Henry Seidel Canby, though they had been part of the Twenties, now, by their attacks in the Thirties on what they called "naturalism," or alternatively "the school of Dreiser," flattered writers like Farrell and Saroyan, Algren and Dahlberg and O'Hara; the genteel mossbacks who had always been opposed to brave new writing were now after *them*.

What young writers of the Thirties wanted was to prove the literary value of our experience, to recognize the possibility of art in our own lives, to feel that we had moved the streets, the stockyards, the hiring halls into literature — to show that our radical strength could carry on the experimental impulse of modern literature. And it was because of this genuine literary ambition that the influence of Malcolm Cowley, then literary editor of the *New Republic*, was so fundamental. For Cowley had lived among the expatriates in Paris, he had just published *Exile's Return* as a chronicle of the lost generation, and each Wednesday afternoon, when I waited with other hopeful reviewers for Cowley to sail in after lunch with a tolerant smile on the face which so startlingly duplicated Hemingway's handsomeness, the sight of Cowley in the vivid stripes of his seersucker suit seemed to unite, through his love of good writing and his faith in revolution, the brilliant Twenties and the militant Thirties. The summer of 1934, that bottom summer when the first wild wave of hope under the New Deal had receded, there were so many of us edged onto the single bench in the waiting room downstairs, so many more of us than he needed for reviews, that Cowley, not knowing what else to do for the hungry faces waiting to see him, would sell

the books there was no space to review and dole out the pro-
ceeds among the more desperate cases haunting him for review
assignments. This kindliness was also a conscious symbol of
the times. Cowley had been at Harvard in the time of Dos
Passos, he had left Harvard in 1917 for service in an American
ambulance unit in the time of E. E. Cummings, he had drunk
in Paris with Hemingway, had fought the *flics* with Aragon,
had walked the Village with Hart Crane. Just as he now lived
in Connecticut (and *Exile's Return* noted when writers began
moving from Greenwich Village to Connecticut), so he was
unable to lift his pipe to his mouth, or to make a crack, without making one feel that he recognized the literary situation
involved. He seemed always to have moved in the company of
writers, literary movements, *cénacles*, to see history in terms
of what writers had thought and how they had lived. When
in his book he recounted his memories of the Dôme and the Se-
lect, hinting at the real names of the characters in *The Sun
Also Rises*, I had an image of Malcolm Cowley as a passenger
in the great polished coach that was forever taking young Harvard poets to war, to the Left Bank, to the Village, to Connecticut. Wherever Cowley moved or ate, wherever he lived,
he heard the bell of literary history sounding the moment
and his own voice calling possibly another change in the literary
weather.

Cowley had more than most the critic's love of writers
and of the literary life, the need to recognize the moment, to
appropriate and to share in the literary feast. And it was this
feeling for movements that made Cowley redirect the literary
side of the *New Republic* in the direction of a sophisticated
literary Stalinism, since for Cowley "revolution" was now the
new stage of development. He had the intellectual elegance
of his generation, and did not indulge the Party-line hacks
for the sake of ideology. In Cowley's reviews and literary es-

says there was no abdication from the standards of the esthetic generation; he wrote of Baudelaire on the barricades in 1848, of Wagner the revolutionary, of Marx's own profound literary culture. Cowley was an expressive poet, and he had such a gift of clear style, he had such distinguished literary standards and associations, he had translated so many books from the French, he had known so many writers and had worked on so many magazines, that I felt in reading him that I had been led up to the most immense spread of literary tidbits. Cowley's face had kept the faint smile of defiance, the swashbuckling look and military mustache of intellectual officers in the First World War, the look of gallantry in sophistication that one connected with the heroes of Hemingway — he even resembled Hemingway in much the same way that matinee idols once resembled Clark Gable; he had an *air*. Unlike the heavy old Germanic progressives from Wisconsin who had just lost their jobs and the professors from Oklahoma fired for liberal opinions whom I met at the *New Republic*, stiffly expectant on the waiting bench; unlike the emaciated and curious English stray who had mysteriously landed on this American beach and looked panicky, starving, wild as he stumblingly tried to get a loan out of the secretaries; unlike the "working-class" writers to whom he passed out review copies with a half-smiling air of acknowledging *their* turn in the literary tide, Cowley radiated ease and sophistication.

Only manic old Joe Gould, the professional Village bum with the little goatee who always went about carrying in a manila envelope what he said was an oral *History of the World*, and who smoked cigarettes through a long holder, ever seemed equal to these periods of waiting for possible review assignments. Gould was literally a scavenger, always so near to starvation that those Wednesday afternoons outside Cowley's office waiting for a book to review represented his nearest hope of a meal. While the others glumly waited and sized each other up, Joe Gould bounced up and down, rushing up to the elderly secretary who coyly cultivated all of us, to make puns in his squeaky high giggly voice. When she dutifully responded to his manic moment of charm, he would grin, turn on his heel, and trot back. Gould came from an old New England family and was a Harvard graduate; he kept secret the fact that he had been a gentleman. I never found him funny; he was a professional puppet for writers in the Village like E. E. Cummings, who condescendingly used him as atmosphere. With his wisp of dirty little beard, his sneakers, his ketchup sandwiches (there was usually a crust of old ketchup on his shirt; it looked like dried blood), his grotesque little inch of cigarette perkily smoking away in his long holder, he looked to me like nemesis. If one waited long enough on the mourner's bench at the *New Republic*, would one get to look like Joe Gould? But he amused Cowley, and certainly he seemed as much a part of the depression as brilliant new revolutionary novels like Silone's *Fontamara* and Malraux's *Man's Fate*, which Cowley reviewed so vividly that I could not wait to get to the key scenes of revolutionary suffering and heroism when I read these books for myself.

The lead review in the *New Republic*, a single page usually written by Cowley himself, brought the week to focus for people to whom this page, breathing intellectual fight in its sharp black title and solid double-columned lines of argument, represented the most dramatically satisfying confrontation of a new book by a gifted, uncompromising critical intelligence. A time would come, in the early Forties, when Cowley could report with astonishment that a famous Broadway designer he had met on the train no longer kept up with these lead reviews;

an era had passed. Cowley was the last of this era — the last *New Republic* literary editor who dominated "the back of the book," and who week after week gave a continuing authority to his judgments. Cowley made his points with unassailable *clarté* and concreteness; he *made* an article each week that one had to read and could remember. He did not have Edmund Wilson's capacity for losing himself in the complexity of a subject; Cowley was always conscious of making a point, and he summed the point up at the end of his review to make sure that the reader got it. He was shrewd, positive, plain, in the Hemingway style of artful plainness that united simplicity of manner with a certain slyness. Whenever you crossed Malcolm directly, he would sidle into his familiar role of the slow-moving and slow-talking country boy from western Pennsylvania, clear-minded and deliberate, definite as the gestures with which he tapped the last pinch of tobacco into his pipe and then looked out at you through the flame of the match as he slowly and puffingly lighted up. But reading his reviews I was stirred by his gift for putting the vital new books into the dramatic context of the times. During the Moscow Trials of the mid-Thirties, when his lead review of the official testimony condemned the helpless defendants accused of collaboration with Hitler and sabotage against the Soviet state, I felt that Cowley had made up his mind to attack these now helpless figures from the Soviet past, had suppressed his natural doubts, because he could not separate himself from the Stalinists with whom he identified the future. To Cowley everything came down to the trend, to the forces that seemed to be in the know and in control of the time-spirit. This gave an unforgettable vividness to his description of the peasants waiting on Silone's door to tell him what had happened to their village of Fontamara, to his description of the wounded Communists at the

end of *Man's Fate* waiting in what had formerly been a schoolyard to be led out by Chiang Kai-shek's soldiers and thrown
into the boiler of a locomotive.

The Communist leaders in *Man's Fate* carried cyanide in the
flat buckles of their belts. The Russian, Katov, took pity upon
two frightened boys waiting to be burned, and in the darkness
made equal shares of the poison and passed them over; one of
the boys was wounded and dropped them. In the darkness, said
Cowley, the condemned searched for the pellets as though
"they were looking for diamonds."

Cowley's review was an exciting concentrate of Malraux,
who was himself an intoxicating concentrate of the pride, vision and sacrifice of those Communists from everywhere who
had been burned alive in China for the greater glory of humanity. Kyo Gisors, the hero of the book, half Japanese and
half French, "had fought for what in his time was charged with
the deepest meaning and the greatest hope." The power of that
meaning and that hope was now reaching me in New York as
I read a book review; exulting in the possibilities of the human
will to a better life, I could not have said what I was excited by
— the vividness of a book review suggesting the power of a
book I had not yet read, dramatizing historical events I did not
fully understand. The critic aroused the reader in behalf of
the imagination that had aroused him, and from where I stood
at the moment, it looked as if the imagination of revolution
and the imagination of literature were stirred by the same
fiery depths.

It was the moment for a great historical myth, and Malraux,
himself still inflamed with the power of Communism to give
creative energy to the heroic will, was read by intellectuals as
the ideal revolutionary novelist. Although *Man's Fate* was politically a bitter criticism of Stalin's policy in China, which in
1927 had ordered collaboration with Chiang Kai-shek against

the better instinct of the Communists who were soon to be massacred by him, this political heresy was not really taken in by those eager to show what Communism could do for intellectuals. Malraux himself had not yet broken personally with the Communists, and his own dominating principle of heroic virtue was that of the committed revolutionary intellectual who serves the Revolution not in the illusion that man is perfectible, but in order to give value to his knowledge of death. Not Communism interested Malraux, but Communists — and only those of a special breed, like Kyo and Ch'en and Katov in his novel, men who had always lived with death as the great idea, and who had to overcome this idea by sacrificing themselves for still a greater idea. Malraux's too-cinematic, portentous descriptions of Shanghai at night showed that he thought of the Revolution as self-help in the minds of intellectual visionaries like himself; his characters were like kings, princes and noblemen who eloquently describe their condition in the set pieces of French classical drama. Yet it was this intellectual, theoretical and consciously Nietzschean sense of the thinker's predicament that attracted Malraux's readers in 1934, though later some of them would use this against him. He was the novelist of the intellectuals' revolutionary *grandeur*. To those for whom society was a metaphor and the instrument of their newly exalted revolutionary will, Malraux was intoxicating, a breath of power.

The condemned Communists in *Man's Fate* — Russian, German, Chinese — embodied the fundamental element of a new religion: they sacrificed themselves. Reading *Man's Fate*, I was led to that dark hall, "formerly a schoolyard," where the leaders of the insurrection lay wounded on the ground, waiting to be burned alive, as pilgrims are led up to the sites of a gallows and a cross. Malraux's underlying preoccupation was that a man prepared to sacrifice his life for a great idea, a cause, his fellows, gives authenticity to his own life; sacrifice absolves the concern with self that the knowledge of our death imposes on us. Sacrifice redeemed the intellectual Communist's inner skepticism, the guilt of his intellectual pride, his unconscious bad faith. The vaguely inflated tone of Malraux's rhetoric, the too conscious demonstration of his own mastery of the situation in Shanghai, 1927, were forgotten in the power of the scene that showed Katov's sacrifice. Malraux seemed to be disparaging his own intellectual vanity in the light of the ultimate seriousness, the terminal question, to which everything else came down: *For what, at last, will you give up your life?* It was a question that a man had to ask himself in a revolutionary era, for he had the choice.

Malraux's Katov was prepared. He chose a terrifying immolation, seized by the necessity of giving his cyanide to two young comrades more desperately frightened of the locomotive boiler than he was.

"Hey, there," he said in a very low voice. "Suan, put your hand on my chest, and close it as soon as I touch it: I'm going to give you my cyanide. There is abs'lutely enough only for two."

He had given up everything, except saying that there was only enough for two. Lying on his side, he broke the cyanide in two. The guards masked the light, which surrounded them with a dim halo; but would they not move? Impossible to see anything; Katov was making this gift of something that was more precious than his life not even to bodies, not even to voices, but to the warm hand resting upon him.

The seriousness of this was overwhelming, and conferred its seriousness — what else was one looking for? — upon the cause for which Katov would be burned alive. And unlike the long procession of Communists soon to be condemned in the Moscow Trials, the many more who were shot without trial, who were to be condemned by Stalin's police in Spain, in the Nazi concentration camps and murder factories, Ch'en, Kyo, Katov in *Man's Fate* were distinct and individual martyrs, their persons cherished in Malraux's text as the saints are cherished by the church. Malraux's novel addressed the future, but the vividness of the leading characters to themselves was rooted in the past. And though official Communist critics pompously complained that there were no real proletarians in it, that was exactly its charm for revolutionary intellectuals who liked "proletarian" as a word but would have been embarrassed by it as a concrete fact.

In Ignazio Silone's *Fontamara*, published here that same burning year, 1934, the peasants of the Abruzzi were not even up to the "proletarian" standard. They were simply and wholly poor peasants, the poorest, living in the poorest and most backward village south of the dried-up lake bed of Fucino, near a broken-down church, dug in upon the back of a stony hill, where a hundred one-story houses, irregular and misshapen, blackened by time and crumbling away from wind and rain, their roofs ill-covered by tiles and rubbish of every kind, were hovels — most of which had only one opening, "which serves as doorway, window, and chimney flue." In the unfloored interior with its dry walls, Silone wrote, "live, sleep, eat and procreate together on the straw matting men, women, and their children, donkeys, pigs, goats and chickens."

Fontamara was "a village mentioned on no geographical map." Its peasants were of such insignificance that their very names — Pontius Pilate, Giacobbe the deaf, Holy Friday — were lumps of earth that the outside world had flung at them in derision. They were not merely ignorant — they were classically ignorant; when the thieving speculator, "the Promoter," offered to share with them rights to the water that was not his to give, they agreed to his proposal that each party should have three-quarters of it. When they went to the Town Hall to inquire into their rights, people were openly frightened of them, and the game warden kept shouting from the window, "Don't let them in here. They'll fill the whole place with fleas." Of all schemes presented to them they felt that "nobody could quite understand it." They were the bottom people, the bottommost people, the most easily deceived, the most exploited. Berado Viola, who was himself so poor that he had no land at all and could not marry, had more spirit than the others and ultimately became their leader, their martyr. Berado warned them never to get into discussions with the boss. "All the troubles of the farmers come from discussions. A farmer is a donkey when he gets to reasoning. That's why our lives are a hundred times worse than those of real donkeys who don't reason (or at least pretend that they don't reason). The unreasoning donkey carries a load of 150 pounds or 200 pounds or 220 pounds; he doesn't carry any more than that. . . . No line of reasoning will stir him. . . . The farmer on the other hand, he reasons. The farmer can be persuaded. He can be persuaded to work beyond the limits of his physical capacity. He can be persuaded to go without food. He can be persuaded to give his life for his boss. He can be persuaded to go to war. He can be persuaded that hell is in the next world."

They never had a parish priest and their church was a shambles. When they got up a petition to the bishop that "our church should have a regular pastor like the rest," the townspeople sent in an old donkey decked out in holy vestments. The only beautiful object in their church was the painting of the Holy Eucharist on the altar, for it showed a piece of white bread, and God was understood to say: "Whosoever hath white bread, hath me." Mocked by the townspeople, ignored by the church, robbed by the Promoter, beaten and their women raped by the Fascist squads when they protested, they were drawn ever more tightly into a net of total misery, oppression and injustice. At the end, when they rebelled and the village had been destroyed, three peasants fled to tell their story to Silone in exile. Their cry, "*What must we do?*", had already answered itself in the self-sacrifice of Berado Viola, who gave his life in jail so that an anti-Fascist agent could go free. It was also answered in the stiff, slow, painfully honest style of Silone himself, holding up the portraits of his *cafoni*, his despised poor, as if to force them upon the consciousness of the world.

What must we do?, the cry first raised in the nineteenth century by Russian writers, and then turned into an agitational question by Lenin, *What is to be done?*, became at the end of *Fontamara* a summons to action through love that Berado Viola embodied in dying for another, Silone in writing his book while sick and despairing in exile. *What must we do?* had meant for Silone, even in 1933, *What must I do?* The very helplessness of his *cafoni* clearly expressed the necessity of some urgent, personal act of solidarity. In the light of *Fontamara*, oppression, misery and injustice took on a luminous quality and became guarantees of response, the ground of human value.

PART TWO 1935

the literary idealism, the note of High Culture, that had been traditional on the *New Republic*.

Ferguson was one of the real roughs of the Thirties — not because he had been a sailor, but because he feared and despised high culture. His jazz, radio and movie pieces, wild monodies called *Nertz to Hertz*, crammed with weird and orgiastic puns, the general razzle-dazzle of his style — all this, wonderful as it often was as force, as farce, as musical sound, was his way of saying *nuts to you, everybody*. He was sour on intellectuals and high thinkers, especially literary ones, whom he sullenly chewed up even when, in duty to the age, he delivered himself of a piece in the *New Masses*. He never tired of making dirty puns on the names of women critics and of playing practical jokes on the literary dignitaries who visited the office. Everything about Ferguson radiated a desire for "kicks," for some ultimate sensation. He had gathered around him, in his brief time on the *New Republic*, a group of *aficionados* who read him with the same physical pleasure with which they listened to certain jazz bands; novelists of the jazz world, like Dorothy Baker in *Young Man with a Horn,* were influenced by his rhythms. Ferguson wrote about literature, in fact, as if it were jazz, and he was always looking in novels for the high sustained note he loved in Bix Beiderbecke, the slang-bang moodiness of the drummer Gene Krupa. He jumped and twitched with the restlessness of a jazz man, and from the moment he came up to you in the corridor, you felt yourself shaking with him, knees, hands and arms jangling in rhythm to some private tune; his mind seemed to be constantly dancing and darting, moving and shaking. It was the flow of this in his writing, this jazzy, shaky, caustic, humming movement in words, that Ferguson's admirers went for. He was the only critic who gave readers the same sensation that they got from listening to jazz, and every true Ferguson piece was a kind of jazz improvisation, blared out late in the evening when the lights were low and the natural melancholy of Ferguson's condition could freely assert itself, wild, all the stops out, words flung out like blaring, sharply colored notes which sooner or later — when Ferguson was in form — mounted to a climax that left the reader exhausted, stupefied with admiration, and happy. The fact that Ferguson could print these arbitrary essays in improvisation was an example of the turnover of standards at the *New Republic*, for its founders in 1914 had been solemn of style and literary gentlemen; even Cowley, who supported him against the timid chief editor whom Ferguson lampooned, gave the impression of being somewhat dazed by Ferguson.

Yet Ferguson, who laughed at all revolutionary intellectuals as impossible utopians and fantasists, was a more revolutionary force on the magazine than any of the good English professors at Smith or the staff critics of *Collier's* and *Time* who were so anxiously militant whenever they wrote a book review for the *New Republic*. Ferguson was a desperate man, a sorehead, a fatalist. Of all the writers I first met in the Thirties, Ferguson was the only one who literally threw his life away in the war; he died in the bombing of his Liberty ship in the Salerno landings, and he was the only man on his ship to die. The last time I ever saw him, one afternoon in 1942 when we were both waiting for our physicals, he said that he was going into the merchant marine to make some money while all the fools were volunteering to write lies for the Office of War Information; he was going to make *money*, he said. Then he said good-by with that sour, snarling, doomed yet vaguely inspiring toughness that he had always worn like a rumpled flag defiant to the last. He was a man who believed in sensations, not ideas; in ecstasy, not communication. I think he was glad there was a war to die in.

*   *   *

One Friday night in the summer of 1935, when I went over to his room to take him out to my parents' for dinner, I found Ferguson working on a piece with a pint of Four Roses at his typewriter to cheer him up, exactly as I had always pictured him when reading one of his wildly plunging pieces — he was honestly loading himself up, like a jazz player, to improve his performance.

Ferguson lived over the old Acme Theater on Union Square, a firetrap that specialized in Soviet films. The Acme was an ancient, narrow, cavernous box dating from the silent days. It was so small that it induced a moving intimacy with the Russian faces on the screen, who seemed lifelike and more "natural" anyway, direct, simple, feeling, angry when they were angry, happy when they were happy, and who could wring your heart as nothing else could when they marched along the dusty road, singing. The way to the men's room was up a narrow ladder just behind the orchestra; the noise of the toilet being flushed could be heard all over the theater. But not until that night had I heard the movie from the floor above. Ferguson, a bantamweight cockily beating time with his heels, was finishing up a piece, humming away at his desk, while the voices of stern and virtuous Soviet military commanders in *Chapayev* boomed up through the floor. "Go it, man!" Ferguson shouted, and grabbing his bottle waltzed it around the room. We were hilarious. The room was loud with the sound of those crunching, nut-cracking Soviet consonants — the very sound of which, when I was down in the theater below, always induced in me so much affection, but which on the sound track alone made you see them as actors carefully molding their voices.

We roared our way down the rickety steps of the building and came out into Union Square. The place was boiling, as usual, with crowds lined up at the frankfurter stands and gawking at the fur models who in a lighted corner window perched above the square walked round and round like bur-lesque queens, suavely showing their coats to the passers-by below and then floating away, haughty and unsmiling. There were the usual "wobblies," as they called themselves, tramps glumly parked at the base of the equestrian statute with their heads down on their chests and their knees up, the usual groups in argument before the Automat, the usual thick crowd pouring round and round the park in search of something, anything, that might be in the stores. There was always a crowd in Union Square; the place itself felt like a crowd through which you had to keep pushing to get anywhere. Suddenly I could not help seeing everything that was habitual to me through Ferguson's jeering mind. He had deliberately taken up residence over Union Square — he had put himself right in the middle of it, sardonically occupying it. He had assimilated himself into my radical, proletarian-bohemian, im-migrant New York without believing in it, out of curiosity and mockery, almost as a joke. And observing the everlasting circle in Union Square Park of people clasped together in argument, the hard summer evening light on the picket line in front of the Kitty Kelly and Beck shoe stores, the immigrant men and women, any of whom looked like my mother and father — the women in flowered loose house dresses, the men in rumpled sports shirts — I saw them through Ferguson's ironic eyes. As he walked through the crowd in his black shirt, his yellow tie, his bright green sports jacket, the stump of a dead cigar in his mouth, he looked like a vaudevillian going to meet his agent. When I saw Ferguson in this jazziest, loudest, most provocative mood, I felt that he was impersonating a vulgarity that was not really his, just as at the *New Republic* he had armed himself against the literary intellectuals by playing the sardonic man of the people. He had encased himself against Union Square in his jazz man's costume. In the park across the street the eternally milling circle of radicals in argument, the crowds always thinning and expanding but never to disappear altogether, seemed to hold the asphalt down.

In order to interest him in myself, I had promised Ferguson an "exotic" meal; I had tried to suggest that in our Jewish cuisine there were mysterious delights which he would never discover for himself, and after a good many postponements I had finally been able to pin him down and to get him to come out with me. All through the long subway ride to Brooklyn on that hot, hazy summer night, while the fans in the subway cars whirred round and round in the too brightly lighted cars, and chewing-gum wrappers and dust blew through the open windows, I seemed to see everything as if I were Ferguson, for I superstitiously thought of him as a visitor from the great literary world. As so often happened with me whenever I was lucky enough to meet anyone who seemed so positive about everything, I automatically tried to switch my mind to his — not because I really valued his opinions, but out of gratitude for my new friend.

It was August, August in New York, and brutally hot. The long subway ride, to which I had always submitted like an Arab slowly toiling through the desert, seemed to me unendurable for Ferguson's sake; and as we finally made our way out into the open and walked through the crowded dark streets of Brownsville to my home, I found myself desperately chattering in order to make up for the silence — and, it seemed to me, the obvious distaste — which Ferguson had put on just getting down the Elevated stairs. I was eager not only to interest Ferguson, but to impress my mother, who with her usual anxiety about our ability to reach the great world wanted concrete evidence, in the shape of a "boss" at dinner, that I was on to something at last. She was nervous about Ferguson's

coming, for she was not sure that a Gentile would like our
food and that she would be able even to communicate with
him. We were all nervous; it was a big night for us. My
mother's unmarried cousin Sophie, who had always lived with
us, had hysterically threatened not to appear at all, for as soon
as she had learned that the distinguished visitor I was bringing
home was not Jewish and still in his twenties, she had miserably eliminated all thought of him as a suitor; the evening had
begun to figure in her mind as an unnecessary ordeal; she could
have nothing to say to him. But her little bedroom was just off
the "dining room" where, for once, we were going to dine, and
as she said, it would have been impossible for her to spend the
evening cooped up in her room while we were all eating and
gabbing away outside her door.

Our cousin Sophie was a difficult case. Because she had
always lived with us, and had often taken care of me as a child
when my mother was ill, I could have thought of her as my
other mother, but she always seemed too young, restless, tor-
mented. Although she was certainly not pretty — her long face
usually looked sad or bitter, and when she was gay, wildly and
almost desperately gay — she radiated, as if it were warmth
from her body, a passionate and angry vividness. All my life I
had seen her, with the long black hair which had never been
cut, her embroidered Russian blouses and velvet skirts, against
the background of a tiny rectangle room scented with musk,
with patchouli, while above the bed covered with a tickly India
spread there hung, side by side, two pictures. One (I learned
their names only much later) was Sir George Frederic Watts's
Hope — a blindfolded young lady with bare feet sat on a globe
earnestly listening for the vibration of the single string on her
harp; the other was Pierre-Auguste Cot's *The Storm*. As the
lovers raced before the storm, their heads were apprehensively
yet exultantly turned back; and the cloak that the godlike lover

was tenderly holding over the woman's shoulders, so light and flimsy that it barely covered her nakedness, seemed woven in its lightness and transparency of "love" itself, so that the gauze veil which together they held over their heads, though too flimsy to shield them from the storm, carried some deeper knowledge of desire that explained the shyness of the woman and the confident and protective smile of the man. As they ran together, just ahead of the storm, they seemed to be running not only under the same veil, but with the same feet.

I had looked at Sophie under those two pictures all my life, just as I had looked at her blouses, her skirts and her petticoats — there was no closet — or could smell from her warm and fragrant flesh, as soon as she came near me, the musk and sandalwood, or could feel her presence again whenever I touched her velvet skirts on the hangers and the stiff crinkly surface of the India spread on her bed. She was never easy with anyone, never tender; there was something about her long sweeping hair and the ungraspable scent of her body that was like the resistance of velvet, which retreats back into itself, in soft and recessive lines, after you have touched it. As a child I had often watched her, while she sat doing her hair in front of the mirror, suddenly in despair let the great mane fall over her face; or else she would sit coldly coiling her hair, doubling and then binding with long black hairpins each sheaf she caught up in her hand. Her moods were always extreme. The whole long day for her was like a sundial, either washed in sunlight or cold-gray in shadow; the moody, somber Sophie, in whose face one saw the control of her despair, alternated with a Sophie reckless, agonized, violently gay, who as she threw her great hair back, or bent over the mandolin with the little black pick in her hand, or coldly stared at some possible suitor stiffly seated at our dinner table whom my mother had hopefully brought in, impressed herself all through my boyhood with

that proud and flashing loneliness that I was to recognize immediately when I first saw *Carmen.*

Sophie was not just the unmarried cousin who had always
lived with us; her unmarriedness, her need of a husband, of
some attachment, was our constant charge and preoccupation.
To this my mother gave as much thought as she did to us, and
at the center of our household, whether she was off in her
room under the picture of the two lovers fleeing from the
storm, or in the kitchen with her friends from "the shop,"
drinking tea, eating fruit, or playing at the mandolin, one
always saw or felt the vividly resentful figure of Sophie —
Sophie beating at the strings of that yellow-shining, deep-
bosomed, narrow-waisted mandolin, Sophie standing in front
of the great mirror in the kitchen combing up her black
black hair. As I watched with amazement, she kept one plait
of hair suspended in her hand and then unceasingly and rhythmically, with the curved comb glistening in rhinestones, drew
it with her long bony fingers through her hair, back and forth,
until, when she had sifted and coiled and piled it up again, she
would gather out the last straggle-thin threads in her hand as if
it were a claw, and with a last sidelong look, manage with one
gesture to throw a little ball of hair away and to give herself
one last approving glance in the mirror. How natural it had
always been to stand behind Sophie and to watch her combing
her hair; or to steal into her room to smell the musk, the
patchouli, the stingingly sweet face powder, the velvet skirts
whose creases seemed still to mark the pressure of her body,
the slips whose straps seemed just to have slipped off her shoulders. In the sepia dusk of the old prints, the lovers still ran rap-
turously before the storm, *Hope* held up her harp, and the
bony gnarled wicker bookstand was filled with romantic English novels like *The Sheik* and Russian novels in stippled blue
bindings which Sophie and Sophie alone could have brought

into the house. And as if the difference had not already been made sufficiently clear between a mother who always seemed old to me and Sophie forever sultry and vivid, it was brought closer by the fact that my mother was at home all day and that Sophie appeared only in the evenings; when she was home, she was often elaborately sick in bed, with a bed jacket, while my mother brought her soft-boiled eggs and toast. The difference in their status was established by the way my mother worked, and waited on her, and told us to be quiet when Sophie was ill; we knew from my mother's constant expression of anxiety over her, from her anguished sulky looks of demanding love, that Sophie lacked something that everyone else in the world possessed.

It was my mother who had impressed all this upon me with an attentiveness, an unremitting anxiety and concern, which from our earliest days had impressed my sister and me with Sophie's special need, with Sophie's unhappiness. For Sophie was unmarried, Sophie needed love: that was what I understood so early about her — so early, when did I not know this about her? When was it not made clear that we were to watch out for Sophie, to look after her, to see to it, somehow, that Sophie's deepest wish might yet be granted, that her life would find its appointed center at last in a husband? When did I not know this, and whenever did we not feel, my sister and I, like juvenile marriage brokers? Although Sophie lived as far as possible from the kitchen, enclosed in her scent, her exotic pictures and books, although she was lodged like a guest deep in the corner room where she would be least likely to be bothered, there was always, behind our tense and tremulous family life, the obligation to look out for her, to be mindful of her special need, to remember that she had some agonizing lack that others did not have, that certainly my mother, by being married, no longer had. Because of this we were always to look out, even on a walk, for someone, for *the* someone, who would give Sophie what she needed, and so take her away. For Sophie was a great sufferer, Sophie was an acute case; she was. a woman who needed love, who throbbed with a special need of love, whose need burned in her, giving her a sultry and splendid fire. This made her figure in my mind as the priestess of some cult which she alone represented. Her need of love went to depths that were her secret, though we were all continually engaged with this need. Loneliness had become her profession. It glowered in her like a passion and was her passion, so that by contrast with her friends from the shop, unmarried like herself, she seemed quicksilver, menacingly alive, radiating heat, a sullen fire, out of the lifelong feeling that she had been deserted.

She was a great sufferer; life had let her down. You could see it in the long pendulous face, stretched into a tense mask of resentful grief, in the bulging eyes constantly trained on you with a look reproachful, flirtatious or demanding. Every encounter with her was personal and intense; even a little boy could feel that it was a love affair to live so near her, for every look that Sophie gave and every look at Sophie herself, as sometimes she lay fully dressed on the India print, staring moodily at the window, had its loverlike strain, its tone and color of feeling, its arousement, its brooding air of possible rapture but present sorrow. All that a man would experience in loving women — the moodiness, the dark excitement, the constant sense of being stretched to new possibilities of feeling — I first guessed at from being near to Sophie. The best of what I ever knew as a child I got from this nearness to Sophie, lay in this brooding, dark, sultry arousement, this sudden brushing of wings, when I felt that it was Sophie, in her insistence on love, in the fierce sullenness with which an immigrant dressmaker no longer young lived for love, that made up the living contrast to my mother's brooding carefulness and distrust.

. With my mother every morsel of life was paid for in fear. You calculated the price of everything before you bought it, and even if you bought it, you could not enjoy it for thinking how much it had cost you. The mark of my mother's character was not caution, which denotes a lack of imagination, but an unrelenting remembrance of our powerlessness, of every hurt, betrayal and sorrow, unquestioning obedience to the dark god, a fearful pledge of grim solidarity with all the forces that had ever molded her and all the people she had ever met. If, at any given hour of the night, my mother happened to wake in pain, her first concern was not with this pain itself, but with pain as the center of a universe all of whose numbers were somehow related to her and for whom she bore distinct responsibility. She could never let go of anything — of no one she had ever known, of no experience. This quality, which anyone could easily have confused with unselfishness, and which made my mother honestly think of herself as a humble sufferer, entirely devoted to others, made her extraordinary in the tension with which she gripped every piece of experience to herself and then imposed it on your consciousness. If, at any hour of the day or night — it did not matter whether she was feeding her children or had been awakened from a deep sleep — someone should mention a Mrs. Bernstein whom she had not seen since the steerage twenty years before, and of whom she knew nothing, not even her first name, my mother would immediately, like a spider, work back and forth on the few threads that connected her with Mrs. Bernstein — she would brood and brood on her, and absorb into the texture of her present sorrow the life story of someone she had not thought of in years.

In my mother's world no one ever shrugged her shoulders;

no one was ever bored or lazy; no one was ever cynical; no one ever laughed. She was an indentured servant of the emotions, and always a slave to other people. This crushing sense of responsibility operated on everyone near her, so that I could never look at a woman well-dressed, proud, sensuous, without instinctively sharing my mother's condemnation of her as frivolous and unkind. My mother was bent, arthritic, and always walked as if she were controlling pain. I seemed always to see her bent to someone's service. Her whole being expressed so momentously her awareness of the grimness of life that one felt that she had taken a solemn oath never to forget it. So deep within her that no actual occurrence could ever modify it, this faithfulness to pain stored in her unrelenting heart every incident, every new occasion of pain, until it, too, became an interior event, an episode in the life of thought.

Later, in the years after Sophie had gone from us, when my mother's anxiety about her became even more acute, I began to see that what held my mother was not her dread merely but the grip of thought on every event, so that life was steeped in care and postponed with infinite considerations. It was from this brooding inner life of my mother's, which in its suffering stubbornness seemed to incorporate the history of the Jews, and was so pledged to permanence that it became her idea of the Eternal, it was from the dread that constantly pressed on her, that I, already stamped with so many of my mother's apprehensions, blindly sought relief through Sophie. She was not only a woman, but a woman who openly and passionately demanded things for herself — who even seemed to be nothing but a demanding self.

If there was one quality about my mother which dominated her, it was her refusal ever to enjoy openly or even to admit that she craved enjoyment. She never ate with us, but waited on us like a servant, handing in dishes from the stove, and after the others had finished, sat at one corner of the table chewing at the leftovers. Yet any day at six Sophie would arrive from the "shop," sulky and complaining of a headache, as if she had spent the afternoon shopping instead of sitting over a sewing machine high above Seventh Avenue, and having been served by my mother, would lie on her bed moodily watching the lights from the great delicatessen sign across the street flashing on her wall while she waited for her friends to come in. They were dressmakers from the "shop" and all unmarried "girls" like herself, who night after night gathered around Sophie in our apartment, made her home their home and always seemed part of our family, for they boarded around the neighborhood. I loved to see them come in any night, for they were gay and careless and affectionate, rich and warm. Whenever they came in the place would sparkle, and even my mother looked pleased as she ran about handing out glasses of tea. Sophie would get positively drunk with excitement. Flushed with joy as she sat at the center of the table surrounded by her friends, her head bobbing up and down like a swimmer racing through the water, her eyes glittering, she bent over the mandolin and flashed the shiny black pick back and forth across the tight steel strings while the polished and ornamented wood of the mandolin reflected the lights hung in the ceiling. In the flashing of her thumb across the strings, in the red faces of her friends sitting too near the stove, and in the songs we sang, I saw that abandonment, that thirst, with which she would give herself, some day, to the ideal loved one.

Surely it was for this look, this possibility, even for her desperateness, that I loved Sophie — for something that said the world is made to be risked, for some sense that our fate is not always to be deliberated. With all the emptiness in our cousin's life, she stood up for herself, she launched herself again and again on those terrible seas — while my mother crept about, silently suffering her bruised and wounded shoulder, eating in her corner after mealtimes like a dog, working every minute of the day as if her life were nothing, as if it consisted in serving others with that same suffering care. Sophie knew that the world owed her something — love, a home, a husband, and from the edge of her bed she waited fiercely, her arms implacably crossed, her bulging eyes mad with rage and expectancy, waiting for *him* to come, for her life to reach its consummation. And while she waited, my mother waited on her, nursed her when she was ill, coaxed her back to life when she was depressed, and all day long, whatever else she was doing, always kept between her tasks the pressing thought to find Sophie a husband, to relieve Sophie of the shame of her unmarried state. I could positively see into my mother's mind as she went about the streets doing her marketing, or buying material for her dressmaking — I could just see her inspecting every likely-looking man who came along, setting traps for every unmarried man between thirty and fifty (so long as he was a Jew and able to make "a nice living") who should happen to pass between Rockaway Avenue and Junius Street on a given day. How many candidates she brought news of before she would even dare bring them back for direct inspection — Sophie listening all the while to my mother's reports with a look on her face scornful and disbelieving, like a princess impatiently being fitted for a gown who cannot make the dressmakers, down on their knees with pins in their mouths, understand how trying they are. And how many were the candidates she actually brought home whom Sophie would stare down at dinner because of some minor awkwardness, like eating too noisily, of which the *chaimyankel*, the poor wretch, had no notion whatsoever as he innocently slurped away at his *borscht*, not knowing that with each spoonful he was digging his grave And how sad it always seemed to me that though

there were a few candidates of whom she could actually approve, and who in turn did feel something for her, the affair
always stopped short, even of friendship. Long after Doctor
Sheshtov, that pleasantly mustached and philosophic dentist
who in his sweet and sage way had allowed her to hope, had
proved to us — all of whom had followed the affair breathlessly, and who had tried to hurry up the courtship by going
to him, only to him, to have our teeth fixed — long after he had
plainly shown that he was not the marrying kind after all, it
was impossible for his name to come up without such a look of
bitterness on Sophie's face that I could no longer pass even
his street without feeling guilty. My mother grimly set her
teeth and openly wished him *six feet underground for what
he had done to our Sophie.*

We were all in it with *our Sophie.* Not an evening ever
passed that Sophie was away at a movie or at a union benefit
with her friends that my mother did not break down at the
kitchen table, and throwing out her arms half in despair, half
in entreaty to God, ask *what is going to happen to our Sophie.*
Not a week ever passed that I was not made to feel by my
mother that the sadness and the loneliness of life were proved
by the fate of *our Sophie,* who, as my mother put it, drifted
about in life aimlessly, to and fro — because she was not
married. Our cousin's life had no *character* to it, no clear-cut
destiny. Let down, let down by life, let down by so many men
who could have married her, who should have married her,
who had promised to marry her, who had acted as if they
would marry her! Our Sophie, our poor abandoned Sophie,
our charge, our weary child, our lonely lonely Sophie! This
was how my mother spoke of Sophie's unmarried state: always
in terms of need, of the great one who would take loneliness
away, of the long loneliness that would be ended by one human being. This was what my own parents had sought in

marriage, for as my handsome father had been an orphan from earliest childhood and my mother regarded herself as ugly and unwanted, they had settled on each other in disbelief that anyone else would love them. My mother once told me how she and my father had made their alliance: they had met in an East Side boardinghouse, they were from neighboring provinces in the old country, they married. And on the Saturday night they married, knowing hardly anyone, my mother had gone out to bring some food back to their room and found my father sobbing. Long before I knew anything else, it seems to me, I knew that people were married because they were lonely, that people had a *right* to get married because they were lonely, that loneliness could be relieved only by marriage, and that without marriage you were condemned to your original and catastrophic loneliness. Lonely you were born and lonely you would die — you were lonely as a Jew and lonely in a strange land, lonely, always lonely even in the midst of people, for my family communicated with each other from loneliness to loneliness, in thought, as I could guess my mother's mind no matter how far away she was. In the end, from my mother's insistence on Sophie's *need* and Sophie's *fate*, I carried away the picture of a woman or man as an abject soul wandering about the world looking for the other — seeking a cloak against the onrushing black sky that one saw in the picture of the two lovers who fled before the storm, running under the same cover, almost with the same feet.

The dinner was not a success. I kept trying to see everything through Ferguson's eyes, and I felt that everything looked very strange to him. For the first time, I had brought into our home someone from "outside," from the great literary world, and as Ferguson patiently smiled away, interrupted only by my mother's bringing in more and more platters and pleading

with him to *eat something,* I tried to imagine his reactions. We
all sat around him at the old round table in the dining room —
my father, my little sister, and myself — and there poor Ferguson, his eyes bulging with the strain and the harsh bright
lights from the overhead lamp, his cheeks red with effort, kept
getting shoveled into him cabbage and meatballs, chicken, meat
loaf, endless helpings of seltzer and cherry soda; and all the
while I desperately kept up a line of chatter to show him that
he was not completely isolated, our cousin Sophie sat at the
table silently staring at him, taking him in. In our boxlike
rooms, where you could hear every creak, every cough, every
whisper, while the Brooklyn street boiled outside, there was a
strangled human emotion that seemed to me unworthy of
Ferguson's sophistication, his jazz, his sardonic perch on
Union Square. But as Sophie sat at the table in her withdrawn
silence, my sister stared wide-eyed at the visitor, my mother
bustlingly brought in more platters, and my father explained
that he had always followed and admired the *New Republic* —
oh, ever since the days of Walter Lippmann and Herbert
Croly! — I felt, through Ferguson's razor-sharp eyes, how
dreary everything was. My father kept slurping the soup and
reaching out for the meat with his own fork; since I had
warned him that Ferguson would expect a drink, he self-
consciously left the bottle of whiskey on the table and kept
urging our visitor all through the meal to take another drink.
My mother, who did not have even her personal appreciation
of the *New Republic* to regale Ferguson with, had nothing to
do but bring food in, and after a while Sophie took to her
room and barricaded herself in.

So the meal which I had so much advertised in advance —
which I had allowed Ferguson to believe would be exotic,
mysterious, vaguely Levantine — passed at last, and after he
had charmingly said good-by to my parents and I walked him

back to the subway at Rockaway Avenue, he studied me
quietly for a moment and said, "What the hell was so exotic
about that?" In order to interest Ferguson in us, I had painted
such delights of Brooklyn and the strange Jewish cuisine that
it now shocked me to realize that from his point of view we
were, as a group, no more exotic or picturesque than anybody
else. My effort to interest him in me by painting us all as if we
wore fezzes, and lived near a palm tree, had plainly not gone
down with Ferguson, who in the office often played the clown
in order to get over the gap he felt between himself and
"literary" people, but who in the ordinary affairs of life had a
common sense that, when I had lost my self-consciousness
with him, more and more impressed me.

As I said good-by to Ferguson at the subway station and
walked through the dark Friday night streets, it unnerved me
to realize that he found us as a group so commonplace. My
first instinct was to seek out a girl I used to walk around with
on Friday nights and find some comfort in her, but she was out
and I walked by myself. In my effort to compass my own
family, to bridge the wall of silence between us, I had always
thought of them as requiring a certain effort to reach. We were
a peculiar set. I was haunted by the lack of intimacy between
my mother and father, and my father's sobs that Saturday
night long ago on the East Side had become my own terror of
being lost. But detached and strained as we all were with each
other — which made every member of my family so "interesting" to me because we were so unreachable — it seemed to me
that we were specially interesting because we were among
the dispossessed of history; I saw us as the downtrodden, the
lonely, the needy, in a way that fitted my faith in a total
redemption.

There are times in history when a group feels that it is at
the center of events. Poor as we were, anxious, lonely, it

seemed to me obvious that everywhere, even in Hitler Germany, to be outside of society and to be Jewish was to be at the heart of things. History was preparing, in its Jewish victims and through them, some tremendous deliverance and revelation. I hugged my aloneness, our apartness, my parents' poverty, as a sign of our call to create the future. I identified everything good with a distant period in time, when my class, my people, myself, would be finally justified. Starting out in the Thirties under people who were "radical," like Chamberlain and Cowley and Ferguson, I could never identify myself with them, for they were so plainly with the haves, with the people who so mysteriously sat in positions of power, for which they had been chosen by — whom? Ferguson's boredom with us, with the crudity that had seemed to me positively sacramental in its significance for the future, with the worldly insignificance of poor Jews from whom had sprung the early passion of Christianity itself, shocked me; it seemed to send us all spinning into a world of actual dullness and tawdriness, where poverty was graceless and Jewishness merely a bore. I did not mind being poor, Jewish, excluded, for I knew that history was on the side of such things; what I could not understand was Ferguson's finding us dull.

At the same time I had a sense of unreality, of doubleness, almost of duplicity, about the daily contrast of my personal life, my friends, my life in Brownsville, with those literary personages in mid-Manhattan who were so exciting and unreal to me that I would come home from a lunch with Chamberlain, or an afternoon at the *New Republic*, in nervous exhaustion. There was a curious parallel for me here with Ferguson, the ex-sailor, who protected himself against the heavily literary tradition of the *New Republic* by emphasizing the boy from Worcester. Ferguson would toss around the new review books as they came in, making visceral puns on the names of literary

gentlefolk like Mary Colum, or attacking the Van Dorens —
who were his special butt, and whom he never tired of lam-
pooning in his jealousy of Columbia professors who wrote so
much and edited so much and knew so much about literature.

I was just then taking Mark Van Doren's graduate course at
Columbia in the art of the long poem, and in the late afternoons
would listen with gratitude to lectures on the *Aeneid* that
brought home, under Van Doren's smiling touch, Virgil's
eloquence and melancholy. Van Doren was unforgettably the
poet in the classroom, direct, full of the most concrete feeling
about Virgil's lines, which he would read with a shy,
straight, Midwestern pleasantness. As the early winter twilight crept over the Columbia campus, Van Doren's craggy
face looked as if he expected the sun to come out because he
was teaching Virgil. He was in such pleasant relation to his
text, his teaching, his students — after the lecture several of
them regularly joined him on the Seventh Avenue local in
order to hear more — he spoke in such accord with the fall of
the lines and the fall of winter outside, that he embodied all
the harmony and smiling charm and love of beauty which I associated with the writers of every generation and place but my
own. All Van Dorens had this particular, "American" and
rhythmical charm, but no one more than Mark at his teaching.
Everything smiled. America was a sweet revolution in itself.
Even in these informal lectures beauty came out of beauty,
and poetry gave birth to poetry; the voice of the poet's eloquence and of the poet's nobility was calm, easy, undismayed
by any terror outside Philosophy Hall.

For Otis, however, Mark Van Doren was just a softy out of
that lying world before the depression. Otis had a whole gal-
lery of the Twenties to shoot at — Benéts, Canbys, Van Dorens,
Christopher Morleys, Alexander Woollcotts, Isabel Pattersons
— cozy, Algonquin-lunching people, people who looked very

individual and literary on book jackets as they were posed with
their croquet mallets against their Connecticut houses. The
more books they published, the more quietly superior the literary judgments they delivered in their chatty literary columns, the more Otis hated them with all the righteous fury of
the sans-culotte who feels that his hour has come. Otis allied
himself to the toughness of the times, to the militant new wind,
to the anger which was always in the air, and in whose name
you had only to point to a soup kitchen, a picket line, the Dust
Bowl, the Memorial Day Massacre in Chicago, to shame those
who had not been sailors like himself, who had not afterwards
worked their way through college like himself, who as writers
were not uncertain, angry and spasmodic like himself. Those
writers of the Twenties, whose faces on book jackets were so
"interesting," picturesque and comfortable, somehow made
books as if they had always lived in books; from childhood on
there had been a protective membrane between them and the
surly crowded streets; they had tidy lives, and so could afford
to despair of the universe at large.

Though I was far more "literary" than Ferguson, I understood this protectiveness. For me, too, all these critics in
power — Cowley, the Van Dorens, Canby, Chamberlain —
were outsiders. Although many of them were also politically
left, it would never have occurred to me then to feel common
cause with someone like Cowley, or to feel particularly close
to Chamberlain, for writers from the business and professional
class could only interpret in an abstract and literary way the
daily struggle that was so real to me in Brownsville. No matter
how radical these critics were, they seemed as alien as J. Donald Adams on the *Times* or Canby on the *Saturday Review*. I
sensed that with them I would have to conceal what I felt
most, for they would have been puzzled by anything personal
that was outside their literary categories. Whenever I got out

after the long subway ride, excitedly clutching a few new books, and walked over to see my neighborhood friends, I felt that I was leaving the stiff world behind, that I was coming home to my own.

It was this rare experience of connectedness in the literary world that excited me the day I met James T. Farrell in his room at the old Brevoort Hotel on lower Fifth Avenue. It was the day in 1935 that Farrell finished *Judgment Day*, the last volume in the *Studs Lonigan* trilogy; on his work table, next to the freshly typed pages of *Judgment Day*, were a Catholic missal and a text of Catholic philosophy by the English Jesuit Martin D'Arcy that Farrell had been using for the scene describing Studs's receiving extreme unction. Although he was obviously feeling triumphant, he looked sharp and unfoolable, he bristled with the intellectual toughness that I was used to, that I expected, in writers of the "people."

There was a young man comfortably draped on the couch who said he was going out to Hollywood to write films, and that he had dropped in to say good-by; he was Nathanael West. He was cool and humorous, lying there with ankles comfortably crossed and his arms under his head, as Farrell impatiently striding about the little hotel room was militant and tough. The visitor kidded Farrell, he was easy, and Farrell — who must have been feeling very good anyway — soon melted and lost something of his professionally tough stance. The toughness disappeared altogether as we got on the open deck of a Fifth Avenue bus going uptown and ran into a young Irish writer who had been trying to meet Farrell anyway, and with whom Farrell was amazingly delighted because the other man's name, too, was Jim. Farrell was pleased with everything now; he was running over, and as he ran over, there was a plaintiveness and unguardedness about him that I recognized and was amazed to find in a writer. For the first time I felt that I was in my own world, and that it had expanded into the creative life — suddenly nothing could have seemed better than this.

When I came to read Farrell's trilogy — *Young Lonigan, The Young Manhood of Studs Lonigan, Judgment Day* — I could not identify any of it with that eagerly melting and touching man so grateful for friendship. I had never read an American novel that was such a furious exposé and rejection of the culture that the author himself had grown up in. Farrell had turned himself inside out, had suppressed every personal attachment, in order to paint, in the starkest, blackest, savagest colors, a culture in which there seemed to be no individuals at all; the center was always the group, the gang, the old bunch on the block, and it rested on the most primitive and brutal reactions of blind loyalty to one's own kind and of savage contempt for everything below.

. . . OOOH, I can't stand the sight or thought of this place and this neighborhood any more. OOOH, to think of all those greasy, dirty niggers around. Every time I pass them on the street, I shudder, Fran said.

Yeah, they look like apes, and, God, you can smell them a mile away, said Lonigan.

Dad, they're coming in here, aren't they? said Studs.

Yeah, a shine offered the highest price for the building, so I let it go. But he paid, the black skunk.

And this is such a beautiful building, Mrs. Lonigan said.

Well, they can have it, only I hate to see how this building and the neighborhood will look in about six more months, said Lonigan.

Yeah, I guess the damn niggers are dirty, said Studs.

I know it. Did you ever look out of the window of the elevated train when you go downtown and see what kind of places they live in. God Almighty, such dirt and filth, said Lonigan.

Sometimes, I almost think that niggers haven't got a soul, said Mrs. Lonigan.

The book was an indictment whose creative force was in the minuteness of detail and in the power of the social logic that he showed in every detail; it was in the pride of assembling these objective social materials and in being able, at last, to bring that dope Studs to the bar of History. In the last pages of *Judgment Day* the extinction of Studs Lonigan, after his idiotic, fruitless life of alcoholism and Fascist hooliganism, contrasted sharply with the parade of young Communists raising their placards while Studs's father, bankrupt, desperate and drunk, angrily watched their happy faces welcoming the future. WE WANT BREAD NOT BULLETS. . . . *Defend the Soviet Union.* . . .

Young Danny O'Neill's kid brother and sister were in that parade. Danny, nearsighted and mad about baseball, to the gang always "goofy young Danny O'Neill," was finally bringing to a triumphant close his trilogy about a petty bourgeois skunk who had always lived in mental squalor, and who did not have the resources with which to survive the crisis of his class. Danny O'Neill was now bringing in to judgment all the punks and slobs, the drunks and rapists, the poolroom bums, gamblers and petty crooks, Weary Reilly and Shrimp Haggerty, Tommy Doyley and Benny Taite, Joe Moonan and Wils Gillen — not one of whom had ever had a thought of his own, and who had gone off by drink, in whorehouses, who had had their brains beaten out on the street. They were all being brought in, at last, by Danny O'Neill, allied with the proletariat, who strode strong and confident to the future down the depression streets of Chicago while his own kind cursed him for a Communist.

What courage it had taken for Farrell to become a revolutionary and a Marxist in that setting, and what a sense of his own personality I drew from his rejection of "personality," of any seeming softness! He had turned himself inside out, I thought in wonder as I read his furiously documented book.

The force of the documentation, the unwearying repetition of ugly, crippling details, had an intellectual ecstasy about it. For Farrell all the lines of force in society pointed to the emptiness and futility of Studs and Studs's kind; they were helpless. The parade on the day of Studs's death, carrying them to judgment, attached all the moral fervor and hope in the world to the author's method. The facts will make you free, said Jim Farrell; look how far they have already carried me! In *Studs Lonigan* Farrell had drawn up his indictment with absolute faith that all the facts were there, that the facts spoke for themselves, that the facts invited only one possible response. He knew what must follow in the mind of the reader once the punks had been brought to the bar of History. Farrell had given his whole mind and heart to an art based on literal truth and to History as the victory of this truth. Some day, he must have said to himself, History will look back and understand the fullness of my hope.

One night I came upon William Saroyan somewhere in midtown. He had suddenly become famous, early in 1934, when *Story* magazine had published the dizzying but lyric account of a young man walking about the streets and dying of hunger, "The Daring Young Man on the Flying Trapeze." Saroyan had lurched into fame out of great misery, confusion, sentimentality and deprivation; he had made it exactly as young writers are supposed to make it, overnight, shooting like a bullet straight from Fresno to New York. And now that he had made it, had come into his own, he was living it up with a wild excitement that paralleled the mad, dizzying rhythms of "The Daring Young Man on the Flying Trapeze."

The story had caught on because of Saroyan's extraordinary dependence on his own feelings. There is no past, he said, and the future is dark; there are no other writers, there are no teachers for us, no examples; there is only me, now, this moment, this crazy alternation of dread and ecstasy. I am alone, and make my writing out of *being* alone; I occupy the streets of the city as I occupy my room and occupy my body: there is only me, going up and down between the dread of becoming nothing and the ecstasy of realizing my kinship with this body, this earth, this space, this moment. One moment it is all dark and nothingness, the next I am whirling out into cosmic space. Words make this possible, but what are words, what is anything? So the reader went up and down with Saroyan, exhilarated one moment by so much independence and let down the next by so much conscious emptiness, yet carried willingly into the shower of words because in some way Saroyan's dependence on his feelings had become the most expressive intimacy with his feelings. Whatever he felt, when he felt it, bounded out into the world, made itself known to strangers, talked of itself in a voice so confiding, sure of sympathy, genial with the expressiveness of its flight, that no one, in a time when so many people were united by the awareness of suffering, could resist the tone in which Saroyan addressed every reader as his brother.

And he was funny in the same hit-and-miss way; he depended on you to understand that he was talking out of himself and by himself. When he went to London he went over to Buckingham Palace and blew his whistle right at it. What was success anyway, or failure? What were words, what was anything but this bright short glow in the dark? "Forget everybody who ever wrote anything," he wrote in the preface to his first book. "Try as much as possible to be wholly alive, with all your might, and when you laugh, laugh like hell, and when you get angry, get good and angry. Try to be alive. You will be dead soon enough."

At the moment, for the moment, he was riding high, and

having met me, just as quickly adopted me. He was staying at the Great Northern, on Fifty-seventh Street, but in a burst of enthusiasm based on our common freedom from Anglo-Saxon convention, he would have nothing to do with cold and ritzy midtown joints and led me up and down cellar restaurants and night clubs to show me all his interlocked Armenian friends and relatives in New York. When we sweatily came back to the hotel, he pressed new Hawaiian shirts on me, wrote long flowing inscriptions to me in his book, and informed me that he was in the chips, he had made it, he was writing the best god-damned new book you ever saw, the only new book with the truth in it, that he was going off to Europe the next day. He was so exuberantly Armenian that he could have been taken for an actor; in that narrow little hotel room, with his shirt off, the bobbing cigar smoking in his mouth as if it were kept lit by the heat in his face, the radio screaming, he looked like a peasant tramping down grapes in a tub. He was wonderful, I was wonderful, the new book was the most god-damned truthful book you ever saw, wonderful! The daring young man on the flying trapeze was now Saroyan, and Saroyan was certainly swinging that trapeze. He was telling me Saroyan, he was preaching me Saroyan, he was impressing the hell out of anyone in sight with Saroyan, Saroyan, Saroyan!

A few days later I had a telegram from him; instead of going off to Europe he had lost the time playing craps, and had ended up in Montana. I had not quite believed that he was going to Europe, and I could not make out if the telegram really came from Montana, but I understood Saroyan's exuberance in public as I understood the Catholic missal and devotional books on Farrell's table. Saroyan wrote as if he had only himself to write from, and Farrell had plotted his book so that Studs's physical collapse would without question symbolize

the logic of capitalism. These were their materials, necessary
to the new writer coming up in the Thirties who really was
of the people — who lived between dread and a wild new hope
that with a book he would create his own life at last. Even in a
New York hotel room Saroyan tried to make you see him as
a tower of strength — and though it was an act, it was no act
to him. Saroyan's insistence that he was strong about everything, his own man all day long, more his own man than anybody else — you bet your life! — was defiance, as he liked
to say, of meaninglessness, uselessness, unimportance, insignificance, poverty, enslavement, ill health, despair, madness. This
exhilarated me.

PART THREE 1936

THE LITERARY PERSON in New York who at that time most clearly brought my two worlds together was V. F. Calverton, who died at forty in 1940. Calverton came from Baltimore, where at twenty-three he had founded his own magazine, the *Modern Quarterly*. In the New York of the Thirties it became the *Modern Monthly;* in his last years it became the *Modern Quarterly* again; and never did the still polemical word *modern* mean so much to an editor and writer as it did to Calverton. He was a round, kindly, swarthy, eager man, curiously distracted, with flowing energy, who wrote

and edited and lectured indiscriminately on sex, on psycho-
analysis, on American literature, on the theory of society, on
anthropology. In his youth he had been a semiprofessional
baseball player, and had thought of becoming a Lutheran minister. Dashing back and forth between Baltimore and New
York, keeping up his magazine singlehanded, writing "social
science" and literature with the same eager knowingness, as if
he were really the heir of Diderot and Bernard Shaw, he nevertheless, for all his bounce, seemed plaintive and absent-minded,
like a man who has unaccountably missed his goal. Calverton
believed that love had to become "modern," and art, and socialism, and criticism, and all knowledge. Everything that a
modern man could learn to believe was to come off the same
great modern tree. The editorial comments in his magazine
were called "the pulse of modernity." Like the great pioneers
of scientific knowledge in the nineteenth century, he moved
confidently from one vast field of learning to another — all on
the strength of his own "scientific socialism." Even close
friends of Calverton's would admit *sotto voce*, at the overflow-
ing parties he was always giving at his Greenwich Village
apartment in Morton Street, that George was lovable "but a
bit of a charlatan." Calverton did not believe he could be pretentious; if he ran thin, it was out of his honest revolutionary
eagerness to put all his intellectual interests on the same locomotive of history. "The complete Socialist," he automatically saw any one idea in productive relation to every other
idea. If he dreamed of mounting "the modern movement"
and on this alone to ride to intellectual glory, it was because
— unlike Diderot, unlike Marx, unlike Shaw — he thought that
a movement could give him all the ideas he needed.

Calverton was someone I knew by heart — there was an
eagerness to impress, a curious willingness to impress despite
his intellectual systemization of everything. When a man op-

erated in every new book, article and anthology by first
"knocking the shackles off humanity"; when his very titles
were *The Newer Spirit, The New Ground of Criticism, The
New Generation, Woman's Coming of Age, Sex Expression in
Literature, The Bankruptcy of Marriage, The Liberation of
American Literature,* who could help liking the positive, hopeful glance he turned on every old subject and every new person? He put me at my ease, he took me up, he brought me directly into his office-home in the house always shadowed by
the great tree on Morton Street, at a time when I had no human
connection with the people I wrote for. As if he were himself
still groping and unestablished, Calverton plainly wanted to
succeed with people, with everyone within reach. He was
available to me as a human being, and I was available for help
with the *Modern Monthly,* which Calverton doggedly kept
alive by borrowing, begging, lecturing and by appealing to
the solidarity of all intellectuals of good will; he could be as
concerned about a new writer's struggles, as hopeful and
friendly about the slightest piece I wrote for the magazine, as
an admiring relative.

Calverton's real name was George Goetz. As a youthful radical in Baltimore, he had adopted a pseudonym in order to keep
his job in the school system, and it was typical of his comfortable, homey side that though he now published everything
under the name of Calverton, everyone still called him George.
Although he came from a solidly German East Baltimore
family, there must have been something about the look on
his face that made people think he was Jewish. When people
asked him straight out if he *was* Jewish, George would smile
but never deny it; there was so much anti-Semitism in the air,
he once said to me, that he could not bear to add to it. With his
enormous curved pipe reflective in his mouth or pondering in
his hands, with his chubby face, the great half-bald dome slid-

ing back to a great mop of hair with an old-fashioned curl, he did look as if he were consciously sitting for his portrait as an amateur Jewish *Philosoph*. George often talked of having ransacked whole libraries as a boy, and he still read books, edited or wrote them, as if they made a meal at the table where, with enormous napkin spread up to his chin, he could be seen bolting them down. He preened himself on being "encyclopaedic," and he had an intellectual vanity, a need to impress, to convert, to take over, that was so familiar as to be positively relaxing. He was the friendliest man and the friendliest mind. It was only his literary instincts that were monotonous. Even when he got on sociological and anthropological topics of which I knew nothing, and on which he talked confidently, I could tell that he was stretching what he knew. I made a willing audience of one, but at the mildest inquiry he would frown and look solemn. He could rattle off names of esoteric authorities in anthropology, ethnology and social psychology like a man who had lived among card catalogues. Every room in his apartment was lined with books from floor to ceiling. In an argument he would invoke the authority of these books with a glance and enlist the very shelves on his side as if he were Samson and could bring them crashing down on his intellectual adversary.

Yet George was hardly a belligerent man. Though his facts went a long way with him, there was something basically humble about the way he trusted to intellectual systems, whether by Buckle, Frazer, Marx or Freud. He particularly wanted to synthesize Buckle with Marx and Freud. He was indefatigably and thoroughly an intellectual Socialist. Evidences lay all around him, waiting to form a system. He could write and lecture on the go because all human phenomena so quickly classified themselves for him; the revolutionary modern centuries teemed with erupting hopes and emerging tools. He was a remarkably unsubtle Marxist critic even for the times, an unflagging grinder of set phrases like "proletarian collectivist" and "decadent bourgeois art." But though existing bourgeois marriage was in bankruptcy, literature at the crossroads, and the times called for a newer spirit, George really did believe that all the "modern" disciplines, sociology and psychology and anthropology, would connect with Marxism to carry all of man to his destiny. The Stalinist critics of the mid-Thirties spoke of *necessity*, but George's favorite word was *liberation*. Just as his assiduous reading had liberated him from the stiff morals of old Germans in East Baltimore, had liberated him all the way to New York and his own magazine and that cool, tree-shadowed house on Morton Street, so he would now liberate the study of American literature from its academic repressions, marriage from its conventionality, society from the oppressions — and Marxist socialism from the Stalinists.

For by the mid-Thirties, when I fell in with him, Calverton was one of the few independently active and prosletyzing Marxist intellectuals in New York who were actually at war with the Communists. He had no faction or party but those independent spirits who, like himself, had been driven off by the Communists, slandered and ostracized by the faithful, for criticizing Stalin's course. Calverton had been a boy revolutionary in Baltimore in 1918, an intellectual sympathizer with the Communists in the early Twenties, when it was still possible to think of them as rebels rather than "shock brigadiers of culture." The early days of Communism were in fact Calverton's Bohemian Period, his Left Bank and his Nineteen-twenties. He was a premature Marxist. By the middle Thirties, when so many respectable and important figures were being welcomed into the United Front and Stalin was being acclaimed as the only responsible leader of the time by reformed cynics on *Collier's* and in many a New York publishing house, Calverton was out of fashion again, this time as a premature anti-Stalinist, and was feeling increasingly isolated.

It was Calverton's personal resistance to the cult of Stalin that I most admired about him; he had been shocked by the cultural authoritarianism of the Communists, and by the time of the first big Moscow Trial, August, 1936, was sickened and outraged by Stalin's frame-up of his old rivals and opponents in the Party. At a time when the literary editor of the *New Republic* was urging intellectuals to accept the official verdict in the Moscow Trials, the *Modern Monthly* rallied every shade of independent opinion on the left against such submission.

Calverton's house, like Calverton's magazine, was a natural gathering place for all sorts of radicals not in the Communist fold — old Russian Mensheviks and Social Revolutionaries, German Marxists who had known Engels and Bernstein, American Socialists and libertarian anarchists, ex-Communists who had fallen off the train of history or had been pushed off it somewhere up the line, possibly in 1921 at the time of Kronstadt, or in 1927 at the time of Trotsky's downfall, or in 1935 with the increasing savagery of Stalin to all former opponents and thus presumably present critics. The *New Masses* could not mention Calverton, Norman Thomas, Max Eastman, Sidney Hook, Eugene Lyons, without accusing them of literary plagiarism, sabotage against the Soviet state, poisoning little children, and any and all other crimes necessary and logical to miscreants opposed to Stalin. But there they all were busily arguing with each other at Calverton's many parties, looking rumpled and all too human against the solid walls of bookshelves, the walls and walls of books whose severe intellectual front engloomed those long and violet-dark rooms put in shadow by the tree outside the house.

The long Greenwich Village rooms humming with darkness, lighted by a few stray lamps, were full of these still separate particles, these old-fashioned scholars who had never joined it and these obstinate rebels who had been thrown off by the Communist machine, which would not tolerate anyone it could not digest. And among the European veterans and American Jews, who looked as if they had made their way to Calverton's house through a mine field, among all the sour, sedentary, guarded faces, were the characteristically lean, straight, bony Yankee individualists with ruddy faces and booming laughs, the old Harvard dissenters, leftover Abolitionists, Tolstoyans, single-taxers, Methodist ministers, Village rebels of 1912, everlasting Socialists and early psychoanalysts, who naturally turned up at George's house as friends of George's own heartiness, his great and open welcome to life. Unlike the European veterans and American Jewish veterans, survivors of many ideological wars, the "Yankees" still looked as unscarred as Norman Thomas and Max Eastman — they looked, indeed, as if they had personally enjoyed resistance to their own stuffy beginnings as ministers or the sons of ministers; they looked as if they had fought down their own kind for the pleasure of fighting. With their open American faces and their frank American voices, with their lean figures and their honest old American instincts, they looked dashing and splendid, undismayed by evil and not afraid to do good. They laughed a lot, even in argument. Norman Thomas's laugh could be heard from one room to another.

At Calverton's there was one horribly experienced Polish veteran of the revolutionary wars, a kindly but despairing expert on all Socialists and socialisms, utopian, scientific, social democratic, libertarian and dogmatic, a man with a heavy bald front and a face shaped like a stone by every obstacle in his path. He had gone through everything, that man, he had

done battle in many factions and groups, and in every country.
He had been through it all — the easy idealism of Socialist
students, the militancy of the Syndicalists, the world-shaking
mystique of the Communists just after 1917 — and he could
never again trust politicians of any stripe. Power corrupted
everyone, and perhaps no one so much as the administrators,
experts, professionals, intellectuals, who sought dictatorial pow-
ers over the working class in the name of their emancipation
from capitalism. The cruelties visited upon the Russian working class in the name of socialism, the deceptions visited upon
the working class in the name of solidarity, the exploitation
visited upon the rulers by the ruled! All was written in the
folds of that magnificent bald dome. Gentle as he was, there
was nothing to ask him, to talk over, that could modify the
tragedy that power represented at all times and in all places,
but never so much as for the exploited who, seeking their
revolutionary emancipation, had put new oppressors to rule
over them from the Kremlin, the Politburo, the Secret Police.
There was nothing to talk over. He would only shake his head.
He had passed beyond all possible illusion. The Russian people
had been oppressed ruthlessly under Czarism; but when they
revolted, it was under the leadership of a small and arrogant
elite of intellectuals, who used the destruction of the old regime
to put themselves, the all-sufficient managers, into the essential
places. There could be nothing in common between those
who worked with their hands, to the last strength of their bodies, and those who sat at desks framing the rules and setting
the pace and giving the orders. Revolution was a tragic cycle:
the powerless, seeking to determine their own fate at last,
gave new power over themselves to ruthless intellectuals.
There could never be any bond between those who worked
and those who ruled. This Polish veteran did not need the big
show trials, just beginning in Moscow, to tell him what he had

already seen of the corruptions made inevitable by power. He had come out of the revolutionary movement an historian of its illusions and catastrophes, its usual renegades and its few, strange saints. He was a living memorial to the futile heroism of the revolutionary movement. For him, socialism had become its past.

Yet this sad, acid detachment was an exception at Calverton's parties. Even Max Eastman, denounced by Stalin himself as "a notorious gangster" and "crook," still believed in the Revolution's positive achievements. Eastman despised dialectical materialism as the "mystical" side of Marxism; for him the Revolution represented a great effort at scientific social engineering, unfortunately diffused with the teleological cant that Marx had absorbed from Hegel. With his mane of white hair, his conscious good looks and his easy laugh, Eastman made his admiration of Lenin's "social engineering" and his contempt for the residue of "mysticism" in Marx's system sound natural, spontaneous, "American." You felt about Eastman that he would have liked, still, to sit down with Marx and talk him out of his unfortunate German tendency to metaphysics — as indeed he had sat down many a time with Trotsky to argue *him* out of the dialectic, much to Trotsky's indignation. Eastman's argument that Marxism had a split personality, torn between its practical scientific realism and its blind Hegelian faith in the final purpose of History, made him sound psychological and therapeutic to it. I had always known of Max Eastman as a romantic poet and rebel, vaguely a male counterpart of Edna St. Vincent Millay, and was not prepared, when I saw him in action at Calverton's parties, for such a steady drumfire in behalf of science, scientific method, experimental naturalism and scientific engineering. When it came to poetry and art he sounded, in the phrase of the time, like a technocrat. His old teacher John Dewey, it seemed, had made a

greater impression on Eastman than anyone else, and the more
he saw his dream of the Russian Revolution receding from
him, the more he called after Marxism to Americanize itself,
to come down to earth, to be practical and sharp, direct and
plain.

Was this Max Eastman the Socialist poet and rebel who had
talked a jury out of convicting him in 1918? Eastman's vision
of the Revolution had been the most intense poetic act of his
life, and the more he saw the curtain of fear coming down on
all the rebels and poets and intellectuals in Russia like himself,
so many of whom had been his friends and intimate comrades,
the more desperately he tried to make the Russian Revolution
sensible, to separate the positive social achievements of eight-
een years from the ominous Stalinist terror. It was his last effort; within a year Eastman would be writing in total rejection
of the Revolution that he had gone with uplifted heart to describe for his friends on the old *Masses* and the *Liberator*. Yet
the fascination of the Revolution was still great, the wild hope
of a totally new society that it had inspired in the minds of
people like Eastman was dying hard. For these thinkers and
scholars at Calverton's house, natural opponents of Stalin the
despot and philistine, there was still more belief in the Revolution than not; its positive value was not yet in doubt. Like
Trotsky himself, they would not believe that "socialism in
one country" meant what it said; the October Revolution,
that nucleus exploding into the twentieth century, could not be
slowed down and its magnificent world-shaking energies
checked that easily! Over their heads at Calverton's house
hung the shadow of the impending Moscow Trials, the destruction of the revolutionary intellectuals, the ferocious terror
designed to whip all elements of the population into perfect
obedience to the State and its Leader; by official decree, in
1935, minors from the age of twelve could be sentenced to

death. Yet obstinately and with ready charm, as if charm could give added backing to his "scientific" arguments, Eastman argued, still, that the Revolution was to be defended, that good sense might yet prevail, if only the expertise of the "professional revolutionary" Lenin could prevail over the messianic side of Marx.

In the *Modern Monthly* there had been a bitter dispute for years between Eastman and Sidney Hook on the scientific value of Marxism. Both trained in philosophy, both disciples of John Dewey, both exponents of "experimental method" and "scientific inquiry," both intensely committed to the practical and moral necessity of socialism, they disagreed bitterly as to the scientific nature of Marxism. Eastman, deploring the "cant" of the dialectic and the "animism" that in his opinion impeded the "scientific straight thinking" of the Marxist analysis of society, ran full tilt into Sidney Hook, who expounded Marxism as a thoroughly scientific, sensibly naturalistic philosophy and a startling anticipation of American pragmatism at its best. Far from wishing to disencumber Marxism of the "metaphysical" idealism that Eastman saw in it, Hook found Marxism an up-to-date and satisfactory philosophy. He approved of it as experimental, naturalistic, thoroughly instrumentalist, and against Eastman's disapproval of the dialectic brought such unsparing accusations of incompetence and of unacknowledged indebtedness to his own more solid studies in Marx's debt to Hegel that before long the two philosophers, the two disciples of John Dewey, were insulting each other up and down the columns of the *Modern Monthly.*

Eastman, almost twenty years older than Hook and over the years distracted from the strict practice of philosophy by poetry, Freudianism, travel, friendship and other pleasures of sense, did not argue as well as Hook. No one ever did. When it came to close argument, Hook was unbeatable; one saw that he could not imagine himself defeated in argument. The concentration of all his intellectual forces upon the point at issue was overwhelming, the proofs of inconsistency on the part of his opponents were unanswerable; to watch Hook in argument was to watch him moving in for the kill. Socrates may have persuaded his opponents, but Hook invariably shamed them. He was the most devastating logician the world would ever see, and as he had no doubt devastated his teachers at City College, so he was now, at Calverton's house, devastating many an independent radical like himself. Eastman was perhaps not so far off in castigating as "metaphysical" the blind faith in historical progress that Marx had carried over from Hegel; in the years to come, certainly, Hook was to blame on the Communist dictatorship a good deal of what Stalin had been able, for his own purposes, to exploit in the name of inevitable progress. But even at this moment it was clear that Hook had turned Marxism into his own kind of philosophy, that he found it acceptably scientific, logical, experimental and naturalistic because he could not uphold anything that was not scientific, logical, experimental and naturalistic. Hook did not see anything in Freud, he did not see anything in religion, he did not see that any imaginative knowledge could be dependably gained from art. What you needed was the philosophy of John Dewey and of Karl Marx, both of which so clearly supported each other in the mind of Sidney Hook; you needed only his kind of rationalism. So the choice was easy. Hook won all the arguments, but since he always had to be right, he did not persuade one that Marx was scientific and rational because Hook said he was.

It was not Hook's logic that impressed me, for it was always partisan reasoning in behalf of Dewey or Marx or other men's ideas; it was his intellectual passion for these ideas. He was humorless, but never petty; obstinate, but not malicious; domineering, but not self-centered. He did not yield to momentary delights and human appeals, as Eastman did. It was his commitment that impressed me. He was a believer. He wanted to change society totally, to overturn disproven ways of thought, to discard all the encrusted superstitions, to give mankind the new chance that it hungered for. When he contrasted the superstitions represented by the old philosophy and the oppressions inherent in capitalism with the instrumentalism that could be the new knowledge and the cooperativeness (through the application of intelligence alone) that could be the new society, he made the choice stark and the issue dramatic. He put clearly before you the logical choice of scientific intelligence over religious superstition, of planning over confusion, of pragmatism over Thomism, of Dewey over Freud. Here was logic, here was science, here was experimentalism. Here were instruments of social analysis that exposed all the contradictions in capitalist society and could give men all they needed for creating a society practical, sensible, harmonious and just. His method, wholly and entirely rational, would become the lever of the revolution. How could one not grasp it? Hook saw every situation so clearly that he concentrated his whole personality into the force of his logic — then wondered why his opponents were so *dumb,* and no doubt honestly regretted that they were.

Calverton, who also liked to think of himself as a scientific thinker, but with interests perhaps too comprehensive for him to settle down to one discipline, was more elastic and benevolent. After 1935, the Communists rode to new influence on the United Front, and hated no one so much as intellectuals like Hook, Eastman and Calverton who still preserved revolutionary ideas in the form of honest personal judgments. The more isolated Calverton felt as the Communists calumniated him, the more parties he gave and the more he sought contact with every independent spirit in the literary and radical world. Suddenly you saw Thomas Wolfe looming like a boy mountain in Calverton's inadequate doorway, crusading journalists like Walter Liggett of Minnesota who would soon be murdered for his exposés of the local political machine, sensitive and skeptical anthropologists like Alexander Goldenweiser who were contemptuous of Marxism, ex-radicals like Eugene Lyons who had gone completely sour on socialism and all its works, a man named Schmalhausen who was a wild imitator of Mencken's assaults on all radical intellectuals, pretentious and otherwise; labor experts, news commentators, student leaders, Harlem poets. Calverton gathered them all in and tried to give an equal welcome to them all. They were all allies and supporters of the modern spirit and possible contributors to the *Modern Monthly*. He could not bear to have any intellectual dispute become personal. Just as he wrote as fast and as much as possible, so he wanted to remain in friendly contact with as many people as possible; he occasionally sent me around, with enthusiastic notes of introduction, to book publishers and magazine editors who did not know him or who flatly disliked him. In his bountiful and hearty desire to keep all channels open, he would even forget how much his anti-Stalinism outraged many a key figure in a New York publishing house. On one occasion he sent me, with the usual flowingly warm note, to a publisher who, as everyone knew, was a fanatic even among Stalinists. He disdainfully read Calverton's letter of recommendation and then looked me over in such silent hatred that I escaped from his presence as soon as possible. For Calverton I was just the sort of literary apprentice, of unimpeachably radical origin, who would share his socialism and help on the *Modern Monthly*. But while I shared some of the opinions and enjoyed working for the magazine, Calverton's real charm for me was the open, direct way in which he exposed his life to me. There was never a time when Calverton, always hard-pressed and working as if he knew he would die in a few years, would not get up from his desk to talk things over. Even when he complained against the Stalinists who were slandering him, there was some surprise in his face and voice that he could have been so mistaken in people. He worked with such impatience that I once saw him composing the first draft of a novel with carbon paper already in the machine. There were all those anthologies, histories, critiques, lectures on sex, on the newer spirit, on socialism. Yet though his books already seemed to me mechanical, Calverton's accessibility and openness were a gift. He concealed nothing, and one of the greatest charms of those long, picturesquely dark Village rooms with a filigree iron balcony overlooking the street, the apartment pervaded by a steady blue twilight from the walls of books and the great tree outside, was the deliciously lissome lady who presided officially over Calverton's establishment as his mistress.

I had never met a *mistress* before, and Calverton's crusading books on sex and "sexology" impressed me much less than did the sight of his marvelously curved and supple girl, who had a faint touch of model's hauteur. One winter day, when I arrived at Calverton's "studio" to read proof on his magazine, I found her draped on a couch at the center of the room — she had a cold — and the sight of her in that room at the back looking out on the frozen little New York garden outside, of the winter light from the back yard turning everything steely and gray into my vision of Paris, of the proud girl lying there in perfect serenity, was the most rewarding experience I ever had reading proof in Calverton's house. There was an odor of herbs from the kitchen preparatory to some "French" dish, there was Calverton writing another book at his desk, there was I doing editorial chores, and there was the girl. Calverton's life was all before me, and I was grateful to be sharing so much of it. Everything about the girl immediately suggested a delicate offering, a subtle power to give pleasure, that contrasted sharply with the steady dates that were the rule in our neighborhood.

For almost four years I had been automatically making my way, every Friday and Saturday night, to a girl named Nora who lived on the edge of East New York. We had met in high school, when she had been a tomboy and the class rebel, the first girl to wear men's shirts, the first to smoke cigarettes, and the first to tell all the rest of us about Joyce and such dangerous new books as *A Farewell to Arms* and *Point Counter Point*. She was a provoking girl, who liked to tell you that she was, and at fourteen she would act out the great bitches in our favorite books, like Mildred in *Of Human Bondage*, with a snarling cockney accent: "You despise *me*, do you, Phillup? Well, let me tell *you*, Phillup. . . ." This made her feel saucy, wicked, and happily remote from "the man and woman thing," which she despised, especially since her parents quarreled all the time. When I was in college and hadn't seen her for a year or so, I was called away one evening from reading Lewis Mumford's *The Story of Utopias* to a summons downstairs at the local pharmacy. Nora and her closest friend had just been thinking of me, and could I possibly come over to the friend's house on Sackman Street and visit them?

That evening, the rain fell heavily through the trees that lined Sackman Street, and as the three of us sat on the dark porch, enveloped in the misty warm evening, I could feel that despite the giggling of the girls and the reminiscent talk about the experimental novels that had been our bond in high school, my future was being chosen for me. In some way that was like my father's experience, I had been chosen — Nora's friend, at seventeen, was already engaged to a dentist-to-be — although there had never been any open affection between us. I had been the most interested audience for her sophistication, and now I was suddenly and unaccountably sealed into an unspoken engagement. Together we went to the movies on weekend nights and to Coney Island on summer evenings; together, after dates, we stood in the hallway of her apartment house, like hundreds of couples in hallways all over the neighborhood, mixing into this unsatisfactory and routine lovemaking the wistful anticipation of a future that would be "secure." She had settled on me without admitting to love, and after so many years of lovemaking in the movies, in the streets, on the Coney Island boardwalk, on the roof, in the hallway, on the landing outside her door, we were as used to each other's requirements as an old married couple. Yet when I was alone and tried to understand how I had entered into this compact, I felt myself pushed by a force as regular as Friday night. The rain dripping down the trees the night Nora had mysteriously decided on me was to rain down all the trees Nora and I fled in the shadows of the bandstand in Highland Park. We never had a place of our own: only the summer of our graduation from college, when both of her parents went out to work, were we ever alone in an apartment. And then, for those summer mornings of love after breakfast, when all the world was working or looking for work, I would walk out to Nora's house in East New York, past the lines of unemployed men and women waiting outside the relief station on Pitkin Avenue, my excitement and my guilt blood-echoing in my ears as loudly as the loud metal clanging of the emptied garbage cans being thrown back on the sidewalk from the garbage trucks and the visceral whine of the pulverizer inside the truck already eating up the garbage, until I could walk up the dirty white stone steps of her house, where the hallways smelled of sweat and the rancid coolness of back yards, and automatically tiptoe my way upstairs, although

I was certain that both of Nora's parents had already gone to work.

There, in the hard-breathing summer morning, we at last had our privacy; there was the greedy lovemaking which sealed our compact, made us marriageable. Marriage would be our communication; we needed nothing but marriage. But at the moment I was just another unemployed college graduate with parents even poorer than her own, who disapproved of me; after we had engulfed each other on the couch Nora would be so outraged by the sight of me reading and writing for non-paying magazines when I could have been making something of myself that she would throw all issues of the *Modern Monthly* out of the window and scream me out of the house. But she always took me back; she had settled on me. On those hot mornings smelling of the summer rot in the back-yards, in the sweetness of the sudden tearing, which felt like weights heavily taking their time to fall, I waited with patient gratitude to know this falling again. Our intimacy was so domestic that I often felt, as I admired her walking around the kitchen in her white cotton slip, that I had had some previous existence in a kitchen, surrounded by women of the same old-fashioned fullness, and that I had now come back to enjoy them. With Nora's parents away, we could play that the house was ours; and on some mornings I would even agree to make the futile rounds of Manhattan publishing houses, radio stations and magazines so that Nora would let me in.

We were playing at marriage, but many of my friends were getting married, and moving in with the wife's family, just as they were busily taking examinations to become civil service examiners and welfare workers. The old neighborhood poets had grown little mustaches, like Jewish doctors and dentists, and had got themselves married to girls older than themselves, with good jobs in the garment district or in the public school

system. At twenty-one and twenty-two, with the usual break-
neck speed of immigrants' children, they were snugly enclosed in matrimony. They were all radicals as a matter of
course, but at the moment it did not help them that history
had promised to be on their side, or that they were too radical
to approve the New Deal and too intelligent to believe in the
Moscow Trials. Bedrock was getting married. Nora, watching
even the most advanced among my friends walking in couples
like the animals onto Noah's Ark, began to fear that everyone
would soon accomplish marriage but herself, and frantically
looked elsewhere. My free-lance life offered no promise of
anything, and I mechanically looked for jobs in places where
I was sure of not finding any; I knew that I would never take a
job that kept me in an office all day.

Through a friendly secretary whose husband was a bartender
at the hotel, I met a retired British Army colonel who wanted
someone to write out his memoirs. He talked without stopping,
but was too impatient to write; he had been excited by the
popularity of Francis Yeats-Brown's *Lives of a Bengal Lancer*
and hoped that he could get off a book that Gary Cooper
would ask Paramount to buy for him. The colonel found it so
easy to talk that he was sure that I had only to take his stories
down. Day after day in the summer heat I sat with him on the
roof of the Hotel Gotham listening to his stories and watching
the unending crowd on Fifth Avenue. In the brilliance of the
noonday sun, with the many-colored flags over the shops wav-
ing it on, that crowd looked as if it had closed ranks around
itself and could never admit another soul. The crowd fascinated
me, for even from the hotel roof, I could see a mass of other
people occupying the street, reaching to the doors, the elevators, the offices, filling every available space with itself, closing
itself up. How did one get in? The retired colonel, getting
vaguer as he heated up in the sun, floated with dreamlike

detachment over the Fifth Avenue scene, his jaw wagging as he remembered incidents of the Indian army that I seemed to have read in books. I suspected him, but more than anything else I hated him for being so irrelevant to the great Fifth Avenue scene at which he glassily stared. I cared nothing for India, whether it was his "*Indya*" or anyone else's, and was not surprised at his sulky complaints that my manuscript never seemed to catch the "flavor," the "lovely times," as he used to call them, that he wanted the book to recall. "Think of it, man!" he growled. "You can have a share of the rights to the film!" But he was unreal sitting on the same rooftop. I was fascinated by theater, for the ripples of feeling that could unite an audience. But all hopes for a killing on Broadway or in Hollywood were a familiar pipe dream, reminded me of a neighbor who had been driven wild by Clare Booth Luce's success with *The Women*, and wanted me to write a play to run just opposite *The Women* and to be called *The Men*. The colonel sat on the rooftop getting vaguer and more unreachable, and did not react even when I lightly parodied *Lives of a Bengal Lancer*. When he ran out on me, he had paid me just enough to buy a tennis racket.

I got a small free-lance job with a Brooklyn radio station, dramatizing episodes from *Pickwick Papers* and the more screechy stories of Edgar Allan Poe, and for a while fancied myself a dramatist, for it seemed to me, sitting high up in the second balcony of the Belasco Theater, watching Julie Garfield, J. Edward Bromberg, Stella and Luther Adler and Morris Carnovsky in Odets's *Awake and Sing*, that it would at last be possible for me to write about the life I had always known. In Odets's play there was a lyric uplifting of blunt Jewish speech, boiling over and explosive, that did more to arouse the audience than the political catchwords that brought the curtain down. Everybody on that stage was furious, kicking, alive —

the words, always real but never flat, brilliantly authentic like no other theater speech on Broadway, aroused the audience to such delight that one could feel it bounding back and uniting itself with the mind of the writer. I wanted to write with that cunning anger and flowing truth; the writer would forget his specialness, his long loneliness, and as he spoke to that mass of faces turning on in the dark, the crowd would embrace him, thank him over and over for bringing their lives out into the light. How interesting we all were, how vivid and strong on the beat of that style! Words could do it. Listening to Stella Adler as Mrs. Berger in *Awake and Sing*, I thought that never in their lives would my mother and the other Brooklyn-Bronx mamas know that they were on the stage, and that the force of so much truth could be gay. Odets pulled us out of self-pity. Everything so long choked up in twenty thousand damp hall-ways and on all those rumpled summer sheets, everything still smelling of the cold shadowed sand littered with banana peels under the boardwalk at Coney Island, everything that went back to the graveled roofs over the tenements, the fire escapes in the torrid nights, the food, the food, the pickle stands in the shadow of the subway and the screams of protest — "I never in my life even had a birthday party. Every time I went and cried in the toilet when my birthday came" — was now out in the open, at last, and we laughed.

How I admired Odets! How grateful I was to Odets! Even his agit-prop play *Waiting for Lefty* bounded and sang, was crazily right in its close-ups, abruptly sent out such waves of feeling that I found myself breathing to Odets's rhythms. Nothing could have been less like the declamatory heroics of German Communist sailors portrayed at the Theater Union, or the gloomy editorials in the "living newspapers" of the Federal Theater Project, where you had only to look at the social dummies parading the stage as "First Man," "Second Man,"

"Woman," "Line of Soldiers," to know that the choreographers of the Social Theater were putting their usual ciphers through their paces again. I especially hated "Line of Soldiers," for this invariably meant that a series of inexpressibly drab, mud-colored uniforms would clank onto the stage, making the peace-loving audience cower as the sharp bayonet points were caught by the spotlight. In the Social Theater, there was never any scenery but platforms, never any particular settings to fit particular people. The platforms were painted dull black, and everything was stark, muddy, awful, a battlefield. *Waiting for Lefty* also had a bare stage, but Odets worked with human samples, not abstractions. A husband and wife were suddenly revealed by the spotlight, and they were talking. JOE: "It's conditions." EDNA: "We're at the bottom of the ocean. . . . We're stalled like a flivver in the snow. . . . My God, Joe, the world is supposed to be for all of us."

Sitting in the Belasco, watching my mother and father and uncles and aunts occupying the stage in *Awake and Sing* by as much right as if they were Hamlet and Lear, I understood at last. It was all one, as I had always known. Art and truth and hope could yet come together — if a real writer was their meeting place. Odets convinced me. The veterans of ideology at Calverton's house had all the logic, but the actors of the Group Theater had all the passion. I had never seen actors on the stage and an audience in the theater come together with such a happy shock. The excitement in the theater was instant proof that if a *writer* occupied it, the audience felt joy as a rush of power.

I had always hoped for this, but now I saw it every day. History was going our way, and in our need was the very lifeblood of history. Everything in the outside world seemed to be moving toward some final decision, for by now the Spanish Civil War had begun, and every day felt choked with struggle.

It was as if the planet had locked in combat. In the same way that unrest and unemployment, the political struggles inside the New Deal, suddenly became part of the single pattern of struggle in Europe against Franco and his allies Hitler and Mussolini, so I sensed that I could become a writer without giving up my people. The unmistakable and surging march of history might yet pass through me. There seemed to be no division between my effort at personal liberation and the apparent effort of humanity to deliver itself. Reading Silone and Malraux, discovering the Beethoven string quartets and having love affairs were part of the great pattern in Spain, in Nazi concentration camps, in Fontamara and in the Valley of the Ebro, in the Salinas Valley of California that Steinbeck was describing with love for the oppressed, in the boilers of Chinese locomotives where Chiang Kai-shek was burning the brave and sacrificial militants of the Chinese Communists. Wherever I went now, I felt the moral contagion of a single idea.

Like most of my friends, I distrusted Stalin and disbelieved in the Moscow Trials, for we had all grown up with the legend of the Russian Revolution, with admiration for Trotsky, respect for Marshal Tukhachevsky's battles against the Poles in 1924, with sympathy for Bukharin's intellectual achievements. We remembered how Karl Radek as a Soviet diplomat in Germany had appealed to the German workers, flinging from his railway compartment revolutionary pamphlets in German to the soldiers lining the tracks; how Trotsky had so brilliantly incarnated himself, amid the flames of civil war, the most revolutionary and dynamic intelligence in a European military leader since Carnot had driven off the enemies of the French Revolution. These men represented the prophets in arms who were our idea of heroic virtue; the charges that such men had plotted with the Nazis seemed to us absurd and disgusting, especially when the Soviet government published the records of the trials. Then we could see how Stalin's procurator Vyshinsky, himself a late convert to Bolshevism, openly bullied the helpless defendants into making the most abject professions of total infamy, total guilt, lifelong error, while Stalin emerged as the Infallible.

"My defective Bolshevism," admitted Zinoviev in his last plea, "became transformed into anti-Bolshevism, and through Trotskyism I arrived at Fascism, and Zinovievism is a variety of Trotskyism." VYSHINSKY: "So you all organized the assassination of Kirov?" ZINOVIEV: "Yes." VYSHINSKY: "So you all assassinated Comrade Kirov?" ZINOVIEV: "Yes." VYSHINSKY: "Sit down." *Vyshinsky to Kamenev:* VYSHINSKY: "So you confirm that you had such a monstrous plan?" KAMENEV: "Yes, there was such a monstrous plan." VYSHINSKY: "You worked out this monstrous plan and confirm this now?" KAMENEV: "Yes, I do." . . . VYSHINSKY: "What appraisal should be given of the articles and statements you wrote in 1933, in which you expressed loyalty to the Party? Deception?" KAMENEV: "No, worse than deception." VYSHINSKY: "Perfidy?" KAMENEV: "Worse." VYSHINSKY: "Worse than deception, worse than perfidy — find the word. Treason?" KAMENEV: "You have found it." VYSHINSKY: "Accused Zinoviev, do you confirm this?" ZINOVIEV: "Yes." VYSHINSKY: "Treason, perfidy, double-dealing?" ZINOVIEV: "Yes."

KAMENEV: "We clearly perceive that we are fighting against the leaders of the Party and of the government who are leading the country to Socialism." VYSHINSKY: "Thereby you are fighting against Socialism as well, aren't you?" KAMENEV: "You are drawing the conclusion of an historian and prosecutor. . . ."

More than twenty years later, I was to hear young intellectuals in Moscow laugh at the show trials of the Thirties,

mystique for me, and our loneliness a definite heroism — we were usually unhappy and always on each other's necks, but I saw us all moving forward on the sweep of great events. I believed that everyone was engulfed in politics, absorbed in issues that were the noble part of themselves. Despite the daily anxiety of trying to get a push up the inhumanly smooth wall of other people's jobs, I felt, with the outbreak of the Spanish Civil War, that the outrage of Franco, Mussolini and Hitler working together was a challenge, not a defeat; I trusted to the righteousness of history. Just as I was trying to break through, so history was seeking its appointed consummation. My interest and the genius of history simply had to coincide. It did not matter how deceitful and murderous Stalin was showing himself to be in the purges; the Soviet Union, a "workers' state" stained only with the unaccountable sins of its leadership, still represented the irreversible movement of human progress. Even Hitler, by his total infamy, obviously represented a *deliberate* attempt to put the clock back; believing that the Jews, and especially Jewish intellectuals, had a mission to humanity, I never wondered why Jewish intellectuals particularly were hated by the Nazis. We were a moral ferment; easy to kill off, but an unsettling influence. Hitler destroyed German democracy, Dollfuss the Austrian Socialists, Franco was destroying the Spanish Republic and Mussolini thousands of Ethiopians: the daily onrush of events fitted so easily into a general pattern of meaning, seemingly supplied by the age itself, that every day was like a smoothly rushing movie of the time — and I loved newsreels, the documentary novels of Dos Passos with their own newsreels, documentary movies, especially now that in tribute to the emergency of the times there were movie houses in Times Square that showed nothing but newsreels. I was as excited by history as if it were a newsreel, and I saw his-

features and where I often spent half the night, people sat glued together in a strange suspension, not exactly aware of each other, but depending on each other's presence. Far off, the screen hung wreathed in cigarette smoke, but sitting in the balcony, sprawling half-twisted out of my seat so as to endure the hours, I sat in the midst of people barking at the screen like seals. The young Clark Gable, playing a commandingly cold-faced butler whom the young heiress naturally was in love with, drew unnatural reactions from the crowd. In certain shots, his very large ears jutted out of his head like a donkey's, and as a few took up an obscene cry, the crowd would clap rhythmically and jeer. In the darkness of the theater, everything was crazily suspended. It was like trudging through mud. Mornings in Times Square, when I rounded the Paramount Theater on my way up to the *Times*, I would fight my way through the enormous crowds lined three-deep up Forty-third Street for Benny Goodman, and wonder why I didn't stay in the movie all day long. I could feel myself just about ready to give up and let go. I could feel the pressure of all those crowds aimlessly filling up Times Square all day long. Everything was suddenly adrift. I would find myself evenings in Communist social halls, surrounded by classmates who had gone "proletarian," who had taken jobs as countermen in cafeterias, and who after scalding their arms in the scummy grease around the steam tables boasted an aggressive "class" hardness that shamed me. They had broken with the studious patterns we had all been raised in; they had given up solemnly trying to inch their way up the ladder. They had broken with the bourgeois world and its false ambitions. In the clattery Satur-day night rumble of dances in old Ukrainian social halls off Second Avenue, I would find myself envying them for swimming with sure strokes on the surface of chaos. I was still trying to fit things together in my own way, and not getting anywhere; the wise types in the Cafeteria Workers' Union *looked* as if they had found the right answer. And they were as easy with girls, passing them around at dances with comradely contempt, as if being militant about everything brought immediate advantages.

PART FOUR 1937

I could never be sure whether he ingenuously believed that he
could reconcile Catholicism with the Party, or whether he was
not playing a game, like other Catholic "Socialists" I heard of
in those days, and pretended to more faith then he had so that
he could bore from within at sodality meetings and luncheons
of the Knights of Columbus. He was prim, pedantic, timidly
observant of all correctnesses, mildly humorous, everlastingly
in tow of an oversized briefcase jammed with index cards on
which he kept, in green ink, the notes for his thesis on Catholic
trade unionism. It was impossible to imagine him leading anything but the life of a scholar, impossible to imagine him
breathing comfortably in any world that was not academic.
Unlike everyone else I knew, he was always most properly
dressed; he looked as if he were on his way to teach a class,
and he articulated his most commonplace thoughts as if he
were in front of a class. Francis's every stiff and shy gesture
proclaimed a being wholly obedient to education. Even the
faint white flakes of dandruff on his shoulders suggested the
chalk marks left on teachers who lived too close to the black-
board. He was the man in our college class most respectful of
books, and since he was surrounded by Jews, most of whom
were radicals, he stood out like an albino.

This was Francis's attraction for me; in his colorlessness he
was an unspeakable relief from everything that had begun to
sour me with its familiarity. And it was his growing liberalism
in his own closed circle, his open lusting after the intellectual
recklessness he found in his Jewish friends, that became the
basis of his affection for me. I was the corrupter who first gave
him H. G. Wells and Kropotkin to read, Thoreau and Whitman and Blake. As he was to say later, I had prepared him for
Marxism by giving him heretical books. But as I was attracted
to Christians, he was attracted to Jews. I never got to meet his
parents in the Bronx, his many brothers and sisters, or the uncle

who taught in a seminary and was reputed to know Hebrew. But many a Friday night Francis could be seen at our table, his cheeks aglow in the light of the Sabbath candles, busily working away at the fish, the carrots, the special white Sabbath loaf, the chicken, the strudel; the light bulbs in the ceiling circled in his thick white glasses, and he looked around with bliss, beaming at my mother and father, my sister and our cousin Sophie. It seemed to mean so much to him to be with us. Although I now felt stuck in our monotonously Jewish world, Francis was so enthusiastic about it that he made me see my parents with somewhat more interest. For baffling as Francis was to my mother, I could now see her through the eyes of someone from "outside" — and what I saw through Francis's eyes made her as interesting as a book. My mother, framed in Francis's sight, had become a proletarian mother in a novel by Maxim Gorky; she was trudging through the snows, on her way to Siberia, for having defied the Czar. All the workers in the Putilov machine works were her sons, and she was magnificently giving them up to the Revolution. But meanwhile it was hard for me to find the church romantic when Francis, with an experienced sigh, was so critical of it; now that he had been put on his way by Kropotkin, who already seemed to him utopian, and H. G. Wells, who was just "an old-fashioned liberal," he was moving with scholarly briskness toward what, in his mild and careful teacher's voice, he called *necessary intellectual realism*. By the time we were out of college, Francis was already a Stalinist, and a very methodical one. He was so quick to enlist on the side of his new faith the intellectual assurance that he had learned in the old that his devotions bored me. He was the pedant as Communist; the science of society was at his fingertips. I was not much interested in Catholic philosophies of trade unionism, especially when, as Francis instructed me, they had been deliberated with the greatest possible prudence and slowness, and were all wrong anyway: see what Lenin had said from his prison cell in 1898 about Beatrice and Sidney Webb's history of trade unionism. Instead of introducing me to the larger world, Francis had taken on all the narrowness of my own.

But we were pals, and although Francis could not enjoy anything in Yeats and Joyce, he was terribly impressed whenever he came on the smallest articles by a friend. Francis believed that you had to pass through many scholarly tests in order to publish: someone had to grant you the authority. The signs of authority would be posted, always, along life's unending highway. Almost anything that had been published carried its tacit authority for Francis, and anything that had been published under auspices academic, legal or governmental, anything officially instigated or blessed, compelled Francis's respect. We increasingly disagreed about the glories of the Soviet system in these years of the big show trials in Moscow. After Tukhachevsky and his fellow marshals had been tried in secret and shot, after Zinoviev and Kamenev had been tried in public and shot, Bukharin and Rykov and Rakovsky, all revolutionary thinkers and leaders we had grown up to respect, were brought up before military judges, and the prosecutor Vyshinsky pleasantly denouncing them to their faces as vipers, snakes, cannibals, revolting traitors, dogs not fit to live a moment longer, they confessed that they had landed at airfields that had never existed, that they had plotted with "Hitler agents" in Norwegian hotels that had burned down years before the alleged meeting — they had done this in order to dismember the Union of Soviet Socialist Republics, to provoke attack on the Union of Soviet Socialist Republics, to take away from the Union of Soviet Socialist Republics the Ukraine, White Russia, the Central Asiatic Republics, Georgia, Armenia. They had done all this in order "to restore capitalism," and to put a little money into their pockets.

For all of Francis's bristling and fuming at the rotten capitalist press, he lived by the *New York Times,* he would have believed the report of his own death if he had read it in the *Times.* And so he was shaken when he read the confessions of guilt quoted in Walter Duranty's dispatches from Moscow, and even more deeply stirred when he read the official transcripts of the trials, so thoughtfully provided in English by the government of the Union of Soviet Socialist Republics in the cases of the Trotskyite-Zinoviev wreckers, the Anti-Soviet Trotskyite Center of Pyatakov, the Bukharin-Rykov-Rakovsky gang of wreckers, murderers and spies.

These trials were held under the auspices of the *Military Collegium of the Union of Soviet Socialist Republics,* and Francis wilted under the power in this mouthful of words. He bent his head under the weight of these official transcripts; it was as if every screaming syllable of hate out of Moscow had been given authority by the military titles of the judges and the judicial titles of the prosecutor and the crushing disdain for the guilty defendants *outside the pale* so loftily expressed by Vyshinsky. Francis could not doubt the reiterative, hallucinatory charges that such people were outside, outside, mad dogs, criminal oppositionists, heretics, unbelievers, seditionists, driven to conspiracy against the state and murder of the leaders because they had gone AGAINST THE PARTY. Isolation had convinced the defendants themselves. It was impossible, Bukharin admitted to the court, for a Communist to sustain disagreement without, sooner or later, moving against Stalin, which meant moving against the regime, against the Soviet people. . . . The logic of his criminality was clear, he said, to the defendant himself, even if it was not clear to some "West European and Ameri-

can intellectuals. . . . These people do not understand the
radical distinction, namely, that in our country the antagonist,
the enemy, has at the same time a divided, a dual mind. . . ."

"For three months," said Bukharin in his moving last state-
ment to the court, "I refused to say anything. Then I began to
testify. Why? Because while in prison I made a revaluation of
my entire past. For when you ask yourself — 'If you must die,
what are you dying for?' — an absolutely black vacuity suddenly arises before you with startling vividness. There was
nothing to die for, if one wanted to die unrepentant. . . ."

These terrible words, which showed the intellectual vise that
Bukharin had been caught in, convinced Francis that Bukharin
had indeed plotted with Hitler agents to destroy the U.S.S.R.
Would *judges* and *prosecutors* have gone to all this trouble if
the defendants had not been caught red-handed? As he believed
Vyshinsky because Vyshinsky was a prosecutor, so he believed
Bukharin because Bukharin was a defendant. Francis believed
that people were authorities on trade unionism, literature, morals, politics, because they published articles on these subjects;
others were authorities on philosophy because they talked philosophy. He was an insatiable collector of authorities, and
whenever he announced that I *had* to meet someone, I knew
that he had found another authority.

The afternoon Francis brought Harriet around to the cafeteria
on Times Square when I was waiting for them, I could feel that
something extraordinary was about to enter my life. I had just
been up to the *Herald Tribune*, and was lost in the excitement
of seeing a long essay of mine on the first page of the *Book
Review*. As I sat there, happily sniffing the fresh ink on an
advance copy, I could see Francis timidly leading in a large
and self-possessed girl, and I had that impending sense of something dramatic that was to characterize all my meetings with
Harriet until the last day I was ever to see her. She had no

sooner come to the table and coolly acknowledged the introduction than she took over. While Francis sat staring at her in
wonder, she looked over my essay, told me that literary criticism was of no significance, and with an engaging grin that
was nevertheless deficient in spontaneous warmth, proceeded
crisply to describe her advanced studies in phenomenology.
Suddenly she sprang up and commanded me to escort her to
an aunt's on Ocean Parkway, where she was staying the night.

I had never met anyone like her. I had never met a *woman*
like her. Not so much tall as big, big with a round baby face
made rounder and more unlikely by the bangs that fitted over
her forehead like a visor, and from underneath which her eyes
gave you a look both pert and inquisitorial, she radiated a hungry self-confidence, an intellectual positiveness, compounded
of her training in philosophy and her superiority over most of
her classmates in the upstate city she came from. Her voice had
a clarion ring. Every syllable struck. Even when she went soft
in girlish giggles or grimaced in mockery, her voice had an
echoing clarity to it. I was astonished, as I went out on the subway with her that evening to her aunt's on far-off Ocean Parkway, that although her cocksureness made me uncomfortable
— up to the end, I was always to feel in Harriet's presence that
she was taking up more space *physically*, in any room we were
in together, than she had a right to, that she was crowding me
off the floor, out of the room, almost off the edge of the earth
— nevertheless I felt happier in her presence, charged with an
excitement that I did not try to account for. Her ambition
seemed to carry everyone else along. The night I met her, she
told me as I said good-by to her in front of her aunt's house
that she was engaged to be married, that she had in fact come
to New York to complete arrangements for the small apartment that she and her future husband had taken on Brooklyn
Heights. Even if I had been comfortable with her, I would

have guessed that I could never be intimate with her; there was an absolute lack of intellectual sympathy between us, while the pleasure I took in her *and* her husband John, as soon as I went down to their room and a half on Brooklyn Heights, was too great.

John, a law student, was the most charming man I had ever met. A natural conservative in a radical period, with a melancholy knowledge of the shoals and traps of human nature, he expressed himself through mimicry, and he could do to a perfection that drove us howling off the couch Franklin D. Roosevelt rather too mincingly denouncing economic royalists, hillbillies on a torrid afternoon lazily discussing with each other the possible need to rescue a daughter who had fallen down the well some days before, pompous Jewish lawyers on Court Street, sailors just off the boat asking directions to the Norwegian Sailors' Home on Montague Street, and the immortal Mr. Lapidus created by the comedian Lou Holtz, Mr. Lapidus who had come to Chicago for his brother's daughter's wedding and had brought the wrong pants. Unlike his wife, who tended rather to instruct their friends, John entertained them. He was strikingly passive, he took things in, he thought them over and waited them out; he let other people take the initiative, but was always more penetrating. Yet together with his wife there was an excitement about them, in that little place on Montague Street, that suddenly brought a new color into my life. There was a wildness that radiated from the militants of the Sailors' Union who seemed always, like myself, in attendance on Harriet, and who brought with them the freshness of New York Harbor two blocks away. I could never get out at Borough Hall and walk down Montague Street to Harriet-and-John's without seeing, in the sudden widening of sea into sky, the enlarging of my life that I connected with them. Montague Street led straight down to the docks, past the little Japanese bridge built over the precipice where the street descended to the piers. At the foot of the street itself, overlooking the harbor, was a circle of benches around a flagpole monument commemorating Washington's successful withdrawal of his troops from the Heights to Lower Manhattan, and there we would sit watching Manhattan Island across the water still seething at night. We would walk down to the piers, stand on muddy little islands near the grass and the orange crates below Brooklyn Bridge, watch as in the half-light the rusty iron lines of the bridge fused in their flight across the river, and then come up the cobblestoned hill from Fulton Street to Columbia Heights, past the bridge between the two Squibb buildings that left shadows in the street, and then up Columbia Heights past the lines of shipping in the harbor, where the hoists made powerful lines in the dark. There was a sense of power that I always felt at the harbor, a deep satisfaction that I had come to the meeting place; there was a throbbing of ships' engines, a watch light in the rigging — and even at night, the constant hammering that I heard as soon as I got anywhere near Columbia Heights. The brilliance of this young couple seemed to lie like a fine gold over the staid brownstones of Brooklyn Heights. In the winter dusk, I climbed out of the subway into the Beacon Hill look of Brooklyn Heights, and in the December dark there were Christmas lights hung over the statue of Henry Ward Beecher, forever lifting up the lowly, freeing the slave girl at his feet. The lights on his shoulders seemed to be bursting, making the street glow.

There were sailors all over the place. On Saturday afternoons, when Harriet served up traditional Sabbath dishes that had been simmering in the oven since Friday afternoon — it pleased her to exhibit as a folk custom what had once been a religious duty not to light a fire on the Sabbath — sailors would walk into the room off the low graveled roof outside. They would heavily tramp their way in to stare at the intellectuals, and Harriet's face would shine in the presence of sailors, she would visibly heat up; the real people were there now. Harriet came from a medical family, she had specialized in philosophy, and in her first weeks in the city, when I often took her sight-seeing on the Third Avenue El, she could never get over the life open to her in bedrooms exposed to the tracks. She saw in the sailor militants from Joe Curran's union every possible hint of the future; they were the virile raw meat which her revolutionary admiration demanded. I was fascinated by her positiveness in all things, her excited discovery of New York, her driving ambition, and although I could not see in these sailors what she did, I identified the clean sea lights and bracing sea airs of Brooklyn Heights with her militant spirit; at night the harbor seemed alive with rigging powerfully walking the ocean floor, the Staten Island ferryboats rocked like toy boats across the soft black waters, and the lighted night windows in the sky-scrapers across the way were blazing cells of thought. Although Harriet seemed to spend much of her time looking for the important place which her gifts would fit, she was herself alive with the age that carried the individual out of himself, that made him feel he was being carried on universal strivings. Her ambition itself came from her certainty; when I proudly introduced editors to her, she would tell them the essentials of philosophy as they dreamily stirred their coffee, and burning with an inner command to give the lead, to show the way, she would recite the history of philosophy as it led up to Karl Marx's *Theses on Feuerbach* — "The philosophers have only *interpreted* the world in various ways; the point however is to *change* it." She identified her scholarly insights with the good of mankind. Yet ambitious as she was, you never felt that she entertained any idea in order to advance herself. In some way that was peculiarly of that time of political and social struggle that was always lifting people out of their personal orbits, she gave the impression that these ideas and convictions, which made her so powerfully unexpected to men, were passionate intellectual absolutes that she took in with her daily food. It was this that created the extraordinary air of positiveness which so many women, who already found it easy to resent her, interpreted as hardness. She had that public soul which in a revolutionary age makes any personal opinion sound authoritative. Her ideas were not merely the most advanced and correct ideas; they were her flesh and blood, and this gave her a feminine force for which many an intellectual was grateful. She had just found a researcher's job on *Time* that compelled her to work the weekend, and on Saturday nights there was always a crowd of friends waiting to take her out for the dinner recess. But if I ventured into her office on the rare day when she openly showed herself at a loss, her fierceness would blow me out again like those winds that rock New York skyscrapers in a storm.

My admiration for her was not reciprocated. She liked intellectuals with a great sense of fact — psychiatrists, biologists, lawyers — and since she had sized me up from our first meeting as someone not clearly useful, I often sensed that I was the tag end of more serious company. Her contempt for the "merely literary" was very much in the style of the period. She had talked herself into a researcher's job on *Time* — an enterprise where women alone could be depended on to organize facts for a "story" and then check their accuracy, putting a dot over each word, after the writer, who had to be male, had handed in *his* copy. The nagging accuracy with which Harriet learned to pin down place names and statistics uncovered her deep affinity with journalistic stories of industrial accidents, medical research, and tribes of pygmies newly discovered in the Amazon jungle. Her office in the Chrysler Building, lined with medical charts, blown-up illustrations from anatomy texts and histories of medicine, surveyed all the other air castles of New York as from a mountaintop. When I sat with her for a minute, buoyed up by the clouds, the spires, the gleams of sugar factories in Queens across the cool silver crest of the East River, I had the sense that Harriet, glowing like the late New York afternoon, had led me up to all these mountaintops.

Harriet was a brilliant success on *Time;* she itched with a feeling for issues. Never as in the Thirties, when history proclaimed itself every day in the significances of daily struggle, could a story in *Time* have seemed so significant to a writer. And Harriet, who soon talked herself into a writer's job, was superbly conditioned for her job because of her own furious impatience for distinction. *Time* was always documenting some great and successful and unparalleled American career with a show of inside knowledge. You saw the great man on his living room sofa, with his dogs; you heard the nickname by which only his fellow ambassadors or corporation executives knew him. Even the writing of a story now became to Harriet a scholarly feat because of the masses of uncollected facts that had to be collected, and a literary feat because of the harsh stylistic frame to which a story had to be fitted. But if you pleased the row of bosses waiting to pass on your copy, you got paid well, praised as only great writers are ever praised, and felt that you were an artist, of sorts. Harriet thought of herself as a writer, not a journalist. She worked as only writers do, and she suffered over each page of copy as only writers do. Even the week's schedule was more a writer's than a journalist's, for Harriet worked Saturday and Sunday, and often stayed up all night on a story. Her tribulations over each assignment might have been Flaubert's over *Madame Bovary;* but with the successful carrying out of a story assignment, especially of a "cover" story, which was the height, the end, the indescribable consummation of all mortal ambition, her reputation advanced among the knowing. Each week she went forth to battle, and each week she had to win. These weekly trials gave the young girl a tense sense of achievement, tinged with anxiety but heady as champagne and the grasp of imperial New York from her window.

John Chamberlain was now on *Fortune*, as were Ralph Ingersoll, Dwight Macdonald, Archibald MacLeish, Robert Cantwell, Louis Kronenberger, James Gould Cozzens; part of the fascination of going up to see Harriet in the new *Time* offices in Rockefeller Center was running into James Agee, Walker Evans, Robert Fitzgerald, John Hersey. Harriet's own intellectual admirations were never writers, and were shifting from sailors to psychiatrists and physicists; these usually had the same harshly left views that the sailors did, but they expressed themselves more suavely. I was so used to people who in any political argument reached for the jugular that the coolness with which Harriet's new friends talked politics surprised and misled me. There was one psychiatrist, with a deep concern for Negroes, who at the same time was positive that Stalin could do no wrong, that Stalin was necessarily scientific about cutting the "cancer" out of Soviet society. In his eyes, the world was most properly run by scientists. He was a scientist, Stalin was a scientist, Marxism was the science of society. Saturday evening after Saturday evening at Harriet's, when she returned exhausted from her labors on the weekly story to a room full of people, I came to see that despite their coolness, some were revolutionaries more fanatical than any of my neighborhood friends, for their opinions rose not from poverty and social despair, but from the pure calculation that existing society was finished. The workers would inherit the earth — if they had the right teachers. These were hard-core Stalinists whom nothing, in the increasingly treacherous years ahead, would ever soften and dislodge.

But Harriet was now racked socially by the same ambition that drove her, a mere woman, to become a writer on *Time*. I recognized that her ambition drove from a natural sense of her own superiority; in a time of endless upheavals and reformings, her personal unrest and intellectual sharpness had to give her first place. Harriet had been the cleverest girl in her family, in the upstate high school and the upstate college, and she clearly thought of herself as cleverer than most people of her generation. Despite the occasional baby face under the bangs and the musical giggles into which she could dissolve, Harriet reacted to any possible competition with the excitement of an actress coming on stage. Yet I was stirred by Harriet's fiercely aching ambition; she was as exciting to be with as the most temperamental actress, and you could never tell what she would come out with. Once, coming back in the subway from a "meeting for Spain" at which André Malraux had described the crucifixion of the country in words that had wrung our hearts, we found seats opposite each other, and when she got up to leave at Borough Hall, she told me that she had been "studying" my face. She liked people to know that she had been "studying" them. She fancied herself a scientific analyst of human nature; she would read to her friends descriptions she had written of them in letters. Yet that evening at Mecca Temple, listening to Malraux describe the suffering and heroism of the Spanish Republicans in stabbing phrases that had driven the agony of Spain like nails into our flesh, she had in emotion given a whole week's salary to the Loyalist cause. At times there was such vitality in her that she would step into a room as if it were some brilliant party which had been gathered to honor her. And this was what excited me most in her; her longing for fame, for intellectual leadership, was so intense, it made her seem passionate and heroic to me. It was like the enthusiasm which makes us forgive the artist his personal savageries and makes us understand his passion for the work. Harriet was like that.

That night at Mecca Temple, Malraux had told the great story, soon to appear in *L'Espoir* and in the film he made of the novel: one of the planes of his volunteer squadron had been brought down among mountain villages behind Loyalist lines. There were no roads down the mountain, only mule paths. Single file, the entire populace followed the stretcher bearers as they brought the wounded aviators down the mountain. At each one of the villages through which they passed, the people were waiting; each village, when the wounded had passed, was emptied of its inhabitants. When those wounded in the face were carried past, the women and children began to cry. And, said Malraux, *"when I raised my eyes, the file of peasants extended now from the heights of the mountain to its base; it was the grandest image of fraternity I have ever encountered."* Malraux also told the story of how, on the first day of 1937, toys sent to the Spanish children from all over the world had been heaped up in the center of the great bull ring in Madrid. Just as the children went to collect them, a squadron of Junkers bombarded the city; they did not come near the ring. But when the raid was over, and the children went back to pick up their toys, none of them, not even the little boys, would touch the toy airplanes, which were left in a heap of their own. When Malraux spoke of the mountain villagers following the aviators down the mountain side, Harriet was literally uplifted from her seat under the storm of his sentences. Although he had to stop every few sentences for the interpreter to catch up, and would draw in his breath like a swimmer, he spoke with such fire that his body itself seemed to be speaking the most glorious French. He was magnificently the writer as speaker, the writer as the conscience of intellectual and fraternal humanity, the writer as the master of men's souls. His rhythms were so compelling that the audience swayed to them. "*We destroyed the airdrome of Seville, we did not bombard Seville. We destroyed the airdrome of Salamanca, but we did not bombard Salamanca. I destroyed the airdrome of Ávila at Olmedo, but I did not bombard Ávila. For many months now the Fascists have been bombarding the streets of Madrid.*" I could hear Harriet beside me drawing in her breath. No figure in the world could have been as magnificent to her as André Malraux was at that moment.

There were times in her new office in Rockefeller Center, as she stood proudly backed up by that blazing, wide-open sky which seemed to go with being an editor of *Time*, when her face would turn red not only with the sun, but also with the intensity of her appetite for the brilliant world that had so many causes. She always led to new places. One warm spring night, in the midst of the Civil War, she took me to the house on lower Lexington Avenue of Muriel Draper, the interior decorator, for another of those "parties for Spain" that were so many in those days. The chic little house, the dear little house out of the old New York still beautifully holding on between Grand Central and Union Square, had a deep alcove in the wall at each landing, and in each alcove a violin stood, tied round in ribbons. This made a gay welcome to the politically advanced members of the Newspaper Guild unit of Time, Inc., who had been gathered in to listen to an appeal for Spain by the British novelist Ralph Bates, who had a particular knowledge of Spain, and who had just returned from the front, where he had been a political commissar. The fashionable in interior decorating made a setting for the fashionable in politics. John Chamberlain shyly and awkwardly introduced Bates, who was the reverse of shy and awkward, and who described the bombings of Loyalist cities in a rapturous style that conveyed his writer's enthusiasm at being able to describe violence so well rather more than it did the tragedy of Spain itself; he spoke with a D'Annunzian exaltation of the fiery breath of war, with a visible relish at being able to find words for the star-bursting shock with which the thud of a bomb reverberated in the brain. All round, blond and English, rosy and compact with English good humor, zest, animal warmth, looking as brisk as if he had come out of a cold tub, Bates stood in the center of the artful Victorian parlor and spoke to a fascinated circle gathered at his feet as if it were an orchestra out of which he was drawing beautiful sounds with a few slight gestures of his hands.

In those days Bates was known as a novelist-adventurer, a restless figure in the tradition of Malraux and Hemingway. He knew Spain well from having grown up in the English sherry trade, he had lived among the Spanish working class, and his novels, full of great literary instinct, were evocative of Mediterranean landscape. At a time when so many English writers were dying at the Spanish Front, Bates also seemed a gallant figure. But he was as a speaker almost dangerously fluent, and was wound up tight to impress his gifts upon every man and woman from *Time;* he was also a Stalinist making propaganda against the Anarchists, Syndicalists and Trotskyites who were being eliminated, on Soviet orders, from political influence. The audience for Bates surrendered to his eloquence, as he meant it to, and solemnly nodded heads when he explained that a political commissar was really "a welfare and morale officer." Bates said that when the Fascists early in the war had reached the outskirts of Madrid, orders had gone out from the Fifth Regiment — the Communist Party's own — for every house in the city to become a bulwark of Spanish liberty. People were instructed to fill bottles with gasoline and plug them with cotton wool, so that at the appropriate moment they might be ignited and flung from windows and balconies against invading tanks and cars. The relaxed and slightly boiled members of the group sitting on the floor gave a cheer. We all cheered. Bates evoked the French Revolutionary spirit of the armed populace in Spain, of the young girls and boys at the barricades, of the old workers fighting hand to hand against the Guardia Civil, which in the first days of the war had dragged workers in Seville out of their houses and knifed them in the street. But Madrid, our Madrid, flesh of our flesh and blood of our blood, all its people one magnificently fighting body now, one voice and one spirit, would push back Franco and his allies Hitler and Mussolini, would on the basis of the sensible policies initiated by the Communists bring the desperately bleeding but magnificently unyielding Republic to victory. Bates was so sure of himself that evening, he spoke with so much conviction, so many ready facts, so much pleasure in his own oral gifts, that he made an almost deliberate contrast with John Chamberlain, who had been awkward and humble in praising him, and who then sat on the floor looking up at Bates with wonder at so much big-city eloquence. The crowd from *Time,* though shaken by the torrent of Bates's words, nevertheless got more genial that unseasonably warm spring evening; Bates unmistakably was somebody, a celebrity, the unusual guest of honor at quite a good party. They were impressed with him, he was bristlingly healthy and many-sided — a novelist *and* a political commissar.

As I went off with her from Muriel Draper's house, Harriet surprised me by speaking with scorn of the society tinge to the occasion. It was typical of her at this unexpected moment that, having been excited by the elegance of the party, she now spoke with bitterness of the shallowness and triviality of her fellow journalists. She broke out, with what was for her a surprising Jewish softness, to praise some science writer on the staff whose impractical manner and shy face had won her affection. Some strange atavistic lament suddenly poured out of her as we walked down Lexington Avenue among the beat-up hotels and seedy stores above Union Square — a piercing loneliness, an unexpected self-accusation at being one in the charmed circle of *Time* editors. Flat little empty people, she called them; no culture, no solid beliefs, no brains! She despised them, she despised herself! She had been eager to advance herself, she had been intellectually eager; only now was it becoming apparent to her that both her ambition and her keenness could be used by people who were utterly smug.

As I was later to see for myself, there was a curiously pretentious show of intellectual "guilt" around the *Time-Fortune* offices, an unnecessary need to show oneself pure and uncorrupted. Professional liberals — not the poet-reporters like James Agee and other gifted writers who were fascinated by the social material of the Thirties opened to them — liked to think that their gifts were misused and exploited; grumbling about the boss made them feel that their wine had not yet turned into Luce's corporate vinegar. There was an affected moral uncomfortableness to liberal and left intellectuals who worked for Luce, a readiness to suffer. Although they were glad of the generous salaries, the constant stir around the place and the travel, they found it necessary to insist that not Henry Luce himself, and above all not Mrs. Henry Luce, could ever control their opinions. Luce had not yet discovered that ours was "the American century" and that John Dewey had killed off philosophy in America; he was an intellectual liberal, of sorts, who had once contributed to the *New Republic* but was now a press lord. His intellectuals found in Luce the convenient image of the liberal turned millionaire. He might own their typewriters, but he would never, never own their souls. The possibility of self-betrayal was as much a convention around Time, Inc. as it was in Hollywood, as much a style as the showy puns and double-entendres by which writers conveyed their intellectual sophistication, as much a habit as the snide, smug and comfortably anonymous malice of Timestyle, which some writers thought of as a demonstration of literary skill. Perhaps writers resented the Luces because they legislated so freely to the whole visible world and thought themselves more than journalists, more than millionaires. But both Mr. and Mrs. Luce had an open love of power and the powerful that made a staff writer who probably agreed with the ideas in Mr. Luce's editorial memoranda and in Mrs. Luce's plays virtuously declaim that these writings were arrogant and hard.

Harriet was becoming restive; her quickness suited *Time* so well that she wanted something more to hope for. She adored working on *Time*, she adored being one of the few women who had moved from the researchers' pool in the back to the imperial front windows of a *Time* editor; her pleasure in her achievement was so great that more than ever it drew people to her with a special force. Yet she had a longing for some special, perhaps nameless distinction that led her, all the time that she was writing for Luce story after story out of her native cleverness and adaptability, to think of herself first as a philosopher and then as a novelist. She was so sure of her value that it killed her not to know exactly where her best advantage lay. She had everything but a form — for she could not accept herself as the skilled journalist she was, she was gnawed by an ambition that nothing would satisfy. Only by feeling "guilty" about something or other on *Time* could she convince herself that she had a greater destiny. She told me this story once. In writing up a horrible industrial accident in New Jersey — a workman had fallen under his machine and had been pressed to death — Harriet, in order to make a *Time* story more vivid, described the victim as so flattened out that he could have been pushed under a door. After handing in the story and departing for home, she was seized in the subway by dismay at her seeming callousness, and returned to Rockefeller Center to correct this impression. She arrived at the office to find that the editor in charge of her column was delighted with it. In telling the story, Harriet's round, large baby face registered horror at the insensitivity of *Time* editors. One was left to suppose that it was economic submission to these forces of corporate evil that explained why she had been forced to postpone her real career as a writer of books.

So far as I could see, Harriet knew only men she was fond of but could not take seriously, and those she looked up to, like the Marxist psychiatrist I often met at her house who would pedagogically enunciate his diagnoses of capitalist society and culture to a Harriet who looked white-faced with ecstasy at the message. It may have been the medical background of Harriet's family, or her own journalizing in the medical field, or the spell of Marxist "science" in the 1930s, but anything scientific or medical always possessed an immediate authority for her that nothing so impressionistic as literature could ever rival. Yet in her ever-charged, gnawing hunger to distinguish herself, she had picked on the writing of fiction as the surest and most direct path to fame; in the unexpectedly few years that remained to her, I never saw her. With her characteristic obstinacy and intensity, she had begun work on a novel about Negroes that seemed to me to have every quality of good journalism. She could never forgive me for not regarding her as an artist.

One Sunday afternoon Harriet, John and I went sailing off a little town on the South Shore of Long Island; the boat belonged to a young student actress whom I had met while doing adaptations of Poe and Dickens for a small radio station in

Brooklyn; she was one of a group of fledgling actors and actresses who were willing to gain "experience" even on those amateurish late evening programs that inevitably ended with the announcer yawning, "This is Station. . . . Anybody listening?" Most of these young and would-be actors had learned a smooth external look before they had learned anything else; they had an air, they strutted, they looked confident. Naomi was small, sallow, nearsighted and intensely quiet. She was a student at the American Academy of Dramatic Arts and from childhood on had planned a career on the stage, yet with her round little spectacled face, her silences, her distinct air of sitting primly in the background observing others, she looked the wardrobe mistress among the flashing young bucks and sports and chattering leading ladies in our small company. Everything about her radiated a humble competence, a modest self-awareness, an old-fashioned decorum and reserve. Yet she was the one professional-minded performer in the group, and she had such personal depth that the self-conscious gestures and facile readings by the others became foolish as soon as she took a part in hand with all her quiet intensity.

Her life, too, was always in hand. Her father was a modestly successful jeweler, and her brother was an equally quiet and competent optometrist. There was an orderliness to her personal existence, a craftsmanlike sobriety and neatness to everyone who surrounded her at home, that made me think of them as the virtuous shoemakers and humble tailors, with square-shaped paper hats, that illustrated old-fashioned children's books. They had a little summer house in the little Long Island town, and a little sailboat. They were quiet and proper and kind. I was often at their house on Sundays, and after the big Sunday dinner Naomi, in blue jeans much too large and bohemian for her, which she seemed to wear to show that she could, would carefully see me into the boat and scrape through a series of small canals, so cut that they looked like a map of her tidy little situation in life, before pushing out into Great South Bay.

Because I often talked of my great friends Harriet and John, Naomi carefully asked me to bring them out one Sunday. We started off with Harriet at the wheel; she was just beginning to drive. Halfway we turned off the Long Island highway because John insisted that Harriet's inexperience was putting us in danger. She turned purple. She was so indignant that John should question her competence at anything that without the slightest concern about what I or anybody else might think, she stood at the side of the road and screamed insults at her husband. After a while, thoroughly exhausted, she sulkily got back in the car and John got us to the small Long Island town where Naomi expected us. Once there, Harriet became charming and wide-eyed, and with her bangs and big baby blue eyes, the coy voice she often affected as a joke, was elaborately and mockingly kind while we sailed about the rest of the day. She was so much bigger and more "artistic" than Naomi, so much the actress, in fact, that she quite hulked over the quiet, withdrawn girl. As so often happened with Harriet in company, she took fire from people not because she liked them but because they gave her a chance to shine, and she was rapturous about the little house, the little boat, the little canals; I half expected her to call our hostess *my little Naomi* to her face. Yet all the while she poured it on, I was not surprised to see her "studying" everything about her with her usual barefaced concentration. On our way back to New York that night she was genial and summed up her findings: Naomi was in love with me, the little girl was not bad at all, we might very well get married.

Harriet managed to suggest Naomi's feeling for me in such a way as to unite both Naomi and myself as equal objects of her condescension. I was not marrying Naomi. I admired her trim competence and her dignity; it fascinated me to watch her take a routine scene of radio melodrama that I had adapted from Poe's horror stories, that depended on the cries, screams, threats that all the others in the company loved to make, but which she would shape to some authentic dimension of character without the slightest attempt to emphasize the hysteria already present in the story. She had worked everything out in her mind — every gesture, every inflection, every rise and fall of tone; and I had a strange intuition that despite her talent she would never become an actress, that she was a thinker, solitary at heart. She was in training for some destiny I could not fathom. I admired her much too much to make love to her; she was externally so ordered, so prim and cool, that despite the silent humor with which she watched the semi-pro gestures of our troupe, I could not help seeing her as the good little daughter of the tidy little home made for her by her sweet little parents. The smooth, regular surface of her life offered no reason for change. On those balmy Saturday afternoons when I would call her out of the apartment near the George Washington Bridge for a walk, the sight of all those trim red awnings gently flapping up and down the hilly streets of Washington Heights emphasized the setting of peace in which I always saw her, and hand in hand we walked along the riverbank, in the shadows of the newly built bridge; our friendship seemed so pleasant and easy that it had no future. There was such easy sympathy between us for which we had not struggled, such an honestly sentimental friendship based on books and music, that it seemed static as well as serene. We were like the afternoons in her parents' apartment, shaded by the red awnings; we were like the even slits of sun on identical brick apartment buildings in the laziness of Saturday afternoons. If we did not talk very much, it was because there were no real hopes to talk about; we never disagreed, and felt a common cause in her ambitions to become an actress and in mine to become a writer; we simply sat together in the warm sunshine of Washington Heights, climbed up the high paths along the river near the bridge, and came back to her apartment for cool sugared drinks. Naomi, so briskly professional as a radio actress, reserved her enormous reserves of sentiment, as we all did, for music that was either Russian wistfulness or Russian militancy. She would sit at the piano playing over and over a song by Lermontov that our cousin Sophie had often sung to her own accompaniment — "*I go out alone upon the road. . . . The stony way glistens through the mist. . . . The night is still. . . . The wilderness is listening to God. . . . And star speaketh to star. . . .*" Then she would immediately switch into *Dubínishka*, the rousing measures of the work gang which had toiled and bled and died — "*But the time it will come, oh brothers, it is near. . . . When we'll rise with an earth-shaking clamor. . . . For the lords and the Czar and the priests, never fear. . . . We will find us a much stronger hammer.*" That was Russia; it always came in two centuries, or two movements: the one plaintive and heart-crushing, the other rousing. Nor could you ever sing one mode without the other, as witness the soldiers in Soviet films as they marched and sang along the edge of the wheatfields where the stalks of wheat quivered like folk song in the throats of the manly Soviet soldiers as they sang. Naomi never tired of these songs any more than I did, and we would see certain movies over and over for the moral exultation of hearing those soldiers sing. That was Russia for you, moral landscape, country of the heart. If on occasion I was so moved by the sad-and-quick of the Russian song that it became unnatural not to embrace her, she would sit up, white-faced and genuinely shocked, at the danger she felt that I was putting her in. Although there was no situation that she could not visualize herself acting on the stage, life was too serious to be mixed up with drama. Downtown, in the ratty little halls where we rehearsed, she saw herself as an actress, faithful to all possible demands of her art; uptown, she lived by her mother's expectations of her, and then she despaired of my bootless life, the shame of that Brooklyn ghetto from which her parents had long before removed themselves. I was just another *Luftmensch* of my beggarly generation.

Naomi was afraid of excitement, of "excess," of any emotion unruly and desperate outside the formal stage parts she loved to recite and the moody Russian folk songs she loved to play; her too neatly cut trimness, her slightly too watchful and wary observation of our troupe at work, all pointed to a prudent wistfulness that wrapped her in a cloud and kept her apart even when she was physically present and working with us. She liked to think that she excepted me from this detachment, but coming back in the subway together from our rehearsals, she would place a restraining hand on me when she felt that I was letting myself go in talking to a friend. Her cautiousness hinted at all the secret disapprovals she would never express. She seemed to notice everything from a remote observation post. But she did not notice everything she could have noticed. She did not notice that the friend across whom she talked to me in the subway was himself in love with her, that he had settled on her.

My friend Herschel had dreams of the stage. There was something too florid about his round body and high bald forehead, which made him look like the actor he longed to be — an old-fashioned actor with a wisp of blond mustache, with pointed shoes that made you look for spats as well, with a velour collar on his overcoat that called for a silver-headed walking stick. But his sense of the drama consisted largely of his using his echoing tenor voice as if it were a wind instrument. He boundlessly admired the voices of actors who were particu-

larly conscious of their voices. He could never believe that Or-
son Welles was just our age, for Welles in his Federal Theater
production of *Doctor Faustus* and of *Julius Caesar* at the
Mercury Theater was so masterful that his face swelled and
brooded over the empty stage like an inflated goblin's. Herschel and I spent a lot of time studying Welles, for he was
more the actor than anyone else we had ever seen, his was the
fat, vaguely crybaby face that was yet the ultimate in stage
Svengalis. His productions usually had no scenery but himself.
The hulking, bullying insistence of his presence was disturb-
ing, fitted in too well with the "revolutionary" rhythms with
which the crowd stormed up and down in his production of
Julius Caesar; Welles played Brutus, and Brutus was a liberal
intellectual in a shabby overcoat plotting against Caesar, who
was a Fascist dictator in a garish Middle European military uni-
form; Brutus was the nervous thread of the action, he was the
conspirator, the assassin, the general, the suicide, whose movements incarnated the disturbance of our time. In *Julius Caesar*
the disturbance was brilliantly brought home; the quick,
alarmed movements of the conspirators back and forth suddenly became a vision of the public anxiety in our minds.

Welles was a quick draught of the lightning we went to the
theater for. In the routine "social dramas" of the time, every
effort was made to shake the audience up, to unnerve it — before sending new hope and determination through it. But
Welles was naturally unnerving. I always felt, when I saw that
too, too expressive face on the stage, that he was trying to impress his own will on the audience, to lead it on a string, to
hypnotize it. We went to anything he did just to see what he
would bring off next. Herschel would imitate Welles as Saint-
Just in *Danton's Death*, Welles as Captain Shotover in *Heartbreak House*, Welles as Faustus dreamily "throwing away"
his great line at the sight of Helen — "*Was-this-the-face-that-*

launch'd-a-thousand-ships?" That voice, that voice! Herschel hoped and trusted that his own voice would yet get *him* somewhere, and as a radio actor was never so happy as when he could imitate a screech owl or an insane murderer. His favorite recitation was as Charles Laughton playing Captain Bligh in *Mutiny on the Bounty*, and stonily defying, from the longboat into which he had just been put, Clark Gable as Fletcher Christian, leader of the mutineers. . . . He would recite this defiant speech in a voice loud and piercing that made the glasses in the room tinkle. As soon as he had concluded, this terrible Captain Bligh would break out in his usual warm smile, rosy with expectation of approval.

Although Herschel was an economist and a Marxist, he had fallen in love with Eliot and Joyce, and found in deciphering *Ulysses* a study that kept his evenings green. His attempts at the stage were exaggerated and often consciously absurd, but he studied *Ulysses* with the patience of a cabalist who awaits the secret of the universe on the next page. The rhythms of Eliot's *Murder in the Cathedral*, sonorously chanted at the Federal Theater, delighted him for the same reason that Joyce's voice did in *Ulysses*. It was interesting to watch this man, who when he did his "part" — his cold cruelty as the murderer Montresor in Poe's *A Cask of Amontillado* — gloried in this chance to be a ham, nevertheless depend on Marxism for all his social ideas, on Joyce and Eliot for his literary faith. With his touching and marvelous belief that someone, somewhere, always had the answer to any problem, he shyly and affectionately put himself into the hands of people who had the answers for him. The spirit of trust that had led him to my room, evening after evening, to talk about *Ulysses*, now led him to put all his love on the silent, reserved and unheeding figure of Naomi. He gave himself, in thought, so completely to this girl that again and again at our rehearsals I would see him white with rapture at the chance to be so close to her. And she, so brisk in her professional obligations, so observant of anything that she could borrow and mimic and use for her parts, so maddeningly cool to him about anything that did not relate immediately to the scene they had been doing together from *Pickwick Papers* — she as the expectant landlady Mrs. Bardell, he bumbly and cheery as Mr. Pickwick himself — never realized for a moment that this same amiably pompous man letting his voice out so loudly could not wait to tell her how deeply he loved her. On the subway coming back from rehearsals, when the three of us were jostling and shaking together on the itchy yellow straw seats, and Herschel was proudly conscious of making a good point before her, it astonished me that she could not see how trustfully this man loved her. I wanted her to recognize Herschel. With touching regard for our friendship, he had even asked my permission to speak to her.

A few weeks later, he did. He went to her and could not wait to tell her that he loved her. Then he came back to my room. He lay on my bed, weeping, and though I sat at my table looking at him in wonder, I also felt a kind of horror. Only once before in my life had I seen someone grieve like that; the day my mother learned of her mother's death in Poland. She had lain on the same bed where Herschel was lying now, she had wept with the same harshness. Looking at Herschel, I thought of my mother weeping that day, weeping as Jews weep in absolute abandonment and without illusion at the death of someone close to them. Herschel, who had never known his mother, was weeping out of the same instinct which had left my father, another orphan, to weep for himself that day in the East Side boardinghouse when he and my mother had arranged a marriage. Loneliness! Loneliness! Everyone I knew talked of love as a shield against loneliness. On this bare ground that held us up under a leaden sky, it was marriage that would save us. When my mother pictured Sophie's fate, it was always in the scary image of someone alone, wasting and dying away because she was alone. Any man who refused her thus became her enemy; he had refused her protection against life. And although Herschel loved Naomi, his feeling for her was still abstract, for he had never seen her alone, he barely knew her. So to see him prostrated with grief after one shy avowal suddenly brought home, from my closest friend, the same commitment to love as one's whole destiny in life that I had lived with year after year of Sophie's languishing away.

Herschel wanted his future clear; we all did. In the day-to-day uncertainty, the young radicals were becoming family-minded, security-minded; there was no place to go but up. The newly trained college intelligentsia rushed into the new welfare jobs, the posts as civil service examiners, that had been opened up by the New Deal in Washington and La Guardia's reform administration in New York, jobs that gave them not only a pay check but a model of the bureaucratic supervision that was their idea of socialism. My friends were going exactly the way of their parents — now that there was nothing to rebel against except their own poverty.

Life was moving fast. One night, another night of rain, like the one on which we had first come together, Nora, standing up against me in her housecoat, indicated that she expected me to marry her. It was something that I owed her — or our situation. She looked pale, beaten and discouraged, very different from the saucy literary tomboy in high school who had introduced me to *Point Counter Point* and *The Sun Also Rises*, who had mimicked the bitch Mildred in *Of Human Bondage* and whose particular way of laughing at everyone had always drawn me. She could not speak of love any more than I could; there had never been any real trust between us; ours had been a gluey neighborhood "relationship." Yet after college she had been able to find nothing better than a secretarial course; as the others married their dentists and doctors, her own parents, who had always been glad to get away to their separate jobs, suddenly woke up to her situation. She was at home all day long. The misery of her days seemed to add up to me. She stood up there against me, more abject than I had ever seen her, passively letting me feel the warmth and fullness of her body in promise of the marriage that she did not really want, she had jeeringly known me too long. And standing there my only thought was that she had become entirely domestic and resigned. She did not want me; she did not know what she wanted — except to be safe, to get away from the chaos that had suddenly gripped her heart when she found herself no longer an impudent schoolgirl, but a pallid and uncertain Brooklyn homebody — unmarried. The pressure of her empty days was too strong.

I knew that I did not want to marry Nora, but a year later, when I heard that she had married someone else, I suddenly felt lost, for it came at the worst crisis that our family had known. Our cousin Sophie, our lifelong boarder, our family charge, our long wept-over and defended and protected old maid of a cousin, was suddenly called for one evening by a man of her own age who had been told of her situation. After talking to her for perhaps two evenings, he persuaded her to pose, "temporarily," as his wife and to go off with him to the Middle West, where he would try to settle into a wholly new career, away from his old job and, as we quickly discovered, from an old wife who would not give him a divorce.

There was the unbelievable, the ridiculous situation that soon turned into screaming tragedy. That a seasoned middle-aged man, presumably in his senses and swaggeringly a man of the world, even conventionally handsome in the heavy movie style of the Twenties, tall, dark, with a glisteningly erotic black mustache, should seek out a miserably lonely, melancholic old maid, already maddened with years of neglect, and after spending just enough time with her to size up her hopeless availability persuade her to *pose* as his wife while they wandered about the Middle West looking for a business he could buy or a job he could get — this was grotesque enough, since the poor woman had done nothing for years but wait anxiously for a man to knock at her door and to fetch her off to distant places. So that when finally he came, the long-awaited, looking so much like what in her wildest dreams she had always desired her lover to resemble, the lover taking her off under his protective mantle, exactly as in the picture of *The Storm* that hung over her bed, the very manner of his coming, and of his taking her off, seemed a fantasy realized. It was all too perfect, unbelievable. And because in his triangular dark good looks he looked like pictures of the devil, I could almost have believed, after the horrible episode had played itself out, that he was the devil. No mere human being could have appeared in our impoverished and insignificant lives like that, out of nowhere; only something maleficent in the very state of things, a concentrated and unresting cruelty, could have led such a man to Sophie at all, could in two days have persuaded her to accept him, and as his new "wife," to accompany him into the unknown and alien West. He had sized her up immediately — even from gossip he had recognized her as the raw material he could bend to any fantasy of his own. The "arrangement" seemed based on the most idiotic concern for the look of things only. The point seemed more to simulate a marriage than to enjoy some middle-aged passion — and all this in the West, where they hardly knew anyone, and to which she would now be going as his coy, awkward, overage "bride."

Her hopelessness I already knew so well that I understood why anyone who came as he came — tall, dark and oily, Ronald Colman mustache, cigarette in hand and little smile on lip — anyone who seemed already to know her heart, would immediately conquer one who no longer needed persuading. By the time he walked in, she had been disappointed by so many dentists and clothing manufacturers that she was quite ready for anybody. But how was it possible, I kept asking myself, that he should recognize her from afar and appear in answer to a silent summons? What did it mean that he should appear like that and use her so thoroughly? Had Sophie's famous loneliness, her constant search for a husband, for the true beloved and savior — had this become such public property that any maniac, looking about for someone as lost as himself, could have heard of her? Was it, as I had seen from so many couples chained in "arrangements," that every human weakness found someone to accommodate it? Preposterously self-possessed and man-of-the-world as he looked to me the first time I saw him, leaning against our kitchen door and surveying us all with the greasy smile of the romantic heavy, he was really more the clothing dummy he resembled when very tired — waxen cheeks, oily black hair and striped suit. He, too, was one of the lost ones, like our Sophie, forever going up and down the world seeking another. Now each found his death in the other.

This much I can grant him now, with both of them so long gone. Putting this story together, I can almost pity him for tying so tightly to her, to pull her after him, the rope that in the end became his noose. But how little we were prepared to consider him. For glad as we were to see Sophie's life wish gratified, even by this masquerade, there was a wrongness about it all that was characteristic of Sophie's life from the beginning; glad as we were to see our "bride" at last depart the house where like so many servant maids we had prepared and anointed her, nevertheless we felt something ominous and unnatural about her going. She seemed fated for fresh suffering.

A few months later my mother went out in a day coach to the state hospital in the Middle West where Sophie lay in a state of uninterruptable shock. He had run off. Not only had he not married her, as perhaps Sophie in the end no longer expected him to — the wife he spoke of divorcing was still in the background, it was all so impossible, she was his fate! — but after months of wandering about the West with Sophie, looking for the business he had talked about in our home with such confident shrewdness, he had become disconsolate and had gone off by himself. We had to guess the rest, for secrecy had been the essence of their affair. She had gone off with him, yet it had not been with *him*, with a man she knew at all; it had been done to impress the "outside," to give the needed look to her life. And what could there have been in that "marriage" of hers but secrecy — the real secret being this man himself? How often did she look at him as he lay beside her, and wonder, in her amazed and terror-stricken heart, who he was at all and why he had come along like a dream? What was he planning, always so busily planning, that he had come out of nowhere to pick her up?

He abandoned her. And finding herself alone now, really alone now, and in strange country, she went out of her head. My mother's name and address were on an envelope in Sophie's bag; this brought her out. Now Sophie was my mother's charge indeed. What a bustle and scatter of preparations there was for the great journey out to the mysterious West that my mother insisted on making, and in a day coach. The afternoon I saw my mother off at Borough Hall for the B & O connection, she was so full of her adventure, going out alone to the West to rescue her abandoned cousin Sophie — my mother, who could hardly speak English and would have to fend for herself with little money in that remote Western land full of strangers! — that there was a jolliness in the air. Sophie's going had broken up many things. My father and I happily ate in cafeterias all week.

Some ten days later my mother returned, full of her trip. Sophie had not recognized her. She never recognized anybody again. She was finally alone with what she had always felt to be waiting for her, and now she was what my mother most dreaded in life. But it took Sophie twenty years more to die, and so, though Sophie was away, Sophie was in fact always with her. Three times a year, year after year, my sister or I would drearily write the same stilted letter of inquiry to the superintendent of the state hospital at B———, to receive in due course the unchanging reply that Mrs. Sophie F———, number 18178, was physically well but in mental condition unchanged. Signed, Dr. ———, Superintendent. I worked in Sophie's room now and slept in Sophie's bed, under George Frederic Watts's picture of *Hope* and Pierre-Auguste Cot's *The Storm.* Whenever we would get the routine reply from the superintendent (at times it carried the plain suggestion that Sophie was physically *too* well), I would remember how beautiful her uncut hair had always been, how her body vibrated as she bent over to strike her mandolin with her pick, and I would shudder at her lying so far off, staring at the ceiling, waiting for death. Year after year my mother, on regularly pronouncing the word *Sophie*, would remember her great trip to the Middle West and weep that Sophie had not recognized her. Sophie had looked at her blankly. "Poor Sophie," my mother often said. "She never had any luck."

ONE SUNDAY in the summer of 1938 I was at a vacation camp upstate, preparing to go in to lunch, when I noticed a girl quietly waiting on the porch. She wore blue shorts and an embroidered Russian blouse, and the pert pigtails standing up from her deep black hair were humorous against a delicately olive-colored Russian face that looked Asian in the concentration of its reserve. That summer day, watching her face in the shadows of the screen door as she stood waiting like a dancer at rest, I felt, as I was always to feel before the perfection and reserve of that face, that I was waiting to see it become what it suggested to my imagination. Her face led me into abysses of nostalgia, into passionate attachment to countries I had never seen and to causes I did not know I believed in. I recognized all the favorite materials of my imagination. It did not astonish me to learn that she had been named Natasha, after the heroine of *War and Peace;* that she was a research bacteriologist; that she lived with a Russian family in Washington Heights, and that her room was full of Russian cigarette boxes, textbooks of bacteriology, Russian shawls, and pictures of Aleksandra Kollontai, Madame Curie and Isadora Duncan. I was falling in love with the embodiment of all my cultural pieties — with intellectual Russia, with science, with *progressive womankind,* but above all with that face, that dear Russian face, that commandingly austere and spiritual and world-historical face that had already sacrificed so much for mankind. From the moment I met Natasha, I was enraptured with all the cultural goods that came along with her — the Russian face, the Russian name, the Russian blouse, the Russian woman and the Russian devotion to causes. An inveterate believer in magic countries of the mind, in that spiritual authority I acknowledged only in certain thinkers and writers and faces, I ecstatically greeted my vision of what a woman should look like, of what a great love could be, and did not trouble myself that her face remained as closed and shut-in as it had been that first summer's day. In her own immense loneliness, she submitted to my enthusiasm, my intellectual pieties, my enraptured discovery that I could now connect with the great world; if she knew how ignorant I was of her own heart, she did not let on; probably she hoped for the best; I was in full flood and my ecstasy carried us both along.

Two weeks later we were married. That Monday morning at City Hall, Harriet and John and Herschel were our witnesses, and when Natasha stood up in her yellow blouse to get married, the only people surrounding her were those she had met through me. Nor did it help that even our waiting to be married by machine on a Monday morning coincided with Harriet's weekly deadline on *Time;* we had to wait a long time to be called up, and as we fidgeted in the pews of the Municipal Chapel, Harriet kept striding out to make telephone calls to her editor. "Wedding!" she quoted him derisively. "Who gets married on a Monday morning!" She looked at us with impatience; we were in the way.

Who ever did get married on a Monday morning, in the fake-churchly gloom of the Municipal Chapel, amid the dust flying off the walls, attended by a friend who could not wait to get off for fear of a deadline? We did. Despite the furtiveness surrounding our wedding, it was a happy morning for Natasha and me, and when we moved into a little two-room apartment on Brooklyn Heights, the clean paint smell of the new house and the sense of being at home with ourselves against the vibrancy of all those streets leading down to Brooklyn Bridge and the harbor suddenly gave our lives serenity, a tremulous unfolding of capacities for happiness. Natasha worked in a hospital laboratory most of the day and then went to Bellevue for classes toward her doctorate; I would spend most of the day in the great sun-filled reading room of the New York Public Library, reading toward the first chapters of a book I had begun, at the instigation of Carl Van Doren, on modern American writing. On Mondays I taught one class at the New School for Social Research on Twelfth Street and would then rush over to the Twenty-third Street branch of the City College on Lexington Avenue to teach another. It would have been simpler and kinder for the chairman of my department at City College to give me another evening, but out of spite, because of my frequent appearance in magazines, he had fixed on the same evening that I taught at the New School. This meant that I would reach Twenty-third Street usually breathless, missing the appointed time when elevators took people up to classes, and then run up five or six flights of stairs to meet the class that had been waiting for me. Natasha and I worked all the time. In the hot summer nights at City College I would "teach" *The Ancient Mariner* or *Adonais* for two and a half hours at a clip with the shirt wet on my back to students who had been working all day long and now looked stupefied with the heat under the glaring lights hung from the ceiling. When I was not writing reviews, marking papers, and reading for my book, I would go over to Bellevue to keep Natasha company while she worked in her laboratory on influenza strains. In her white laboratory coat, her glasses, the dark neatly gathered bun of black hair bent over her microscope, she made such a tenderly appealing figure that I would rush across the laboratory to hug her while the white mice raced around their cages.

It was a happy time. I was in a constant state of arousement because of my book; and reading novels by Howells and James, I became watchful to the look and style of their time. After a morning at the shining yellow tables in the reading room of the library that smelled of lemony polish and library bindings, and in which the crinkle of the tissue over the frontispieces in forgotten novels of the period made me hear the rustle of floor-length dresses pictured in the illustrations themselves, I would walk down the grand staircase on my way out to the Automat across Fifth Avenue with gratitude that I was still in the period I had been excitedly absorbing all day. I had fallen in love with the Eighties and Nineties, with the dark seedtime of modern writers and modern art. Just as I found the traces of forgotten time in the beautiful wooden paneling, the high ceilings and the portraits of bearded old New York founders in the halls of the great library itself, so getting off the subway at Borough Hall to walk home I would feel in the dusky downtown Brooklyn

streets, jammed with traffic for Brooklyn Bridge and lined with
old brownstones, old churches, old antiquary societies, old in-
surance offices and courthouses and street clocks, that I had
providentially made my way to my favorite corner of the past.
The downtown Brooklyn streets were a dark grid of El lines,
ancient office buildings fit for the heroes of Oliver Optic,
courthouses built to the taste of Boss Tweed; there was a constant baying from the freighters tied up at the foot of Columbia Heights; and on Sunday mornings, when Natasha and I
walked down Remsen Street to the lookout over the harbor,
making our way there past the old Japanese bridge that arched
Montague Street, past a line of solid mansions with golden oak
doors with glass inserts where fruits falling from a cornucopia
were pictured on the glass as if engraved there in fine needle-
point, our intensely scholarly and decorous life found its natural home in the Sunday peace of old Brooklyn city. Sunday
afternoons, we attended New Friends of Music concerts at
Town Hall where newly arrived Viennese Jews played Schubert and Beethoven and Brahms to breathlessly respectful refugees who listened as if Town Hall were the only part of America they could trust. Our marriage was presided over by Artur
Schnabel and Karl Ulrich Schnabel playing the Schubert Fan-
tasia in F Minor for four hands, by Joseph Szigeti at the
People's Concerts at Washington Irving High School playing
the Bach Chaconne with so much intellectual passion that the
audience seemed to follow from heartbeat to heartbeat, by the
Budapest Quartet playing Beethoven's Opus 132. On Sunday
nights, after Natasha and I had made up the sofa bed in our
living room, we listened to the César Franck Sonata, to the
Glyndebourne Festival recording of *Don Giovanni*, to Schnabel playing the *Waldstein*. Across the street, on the Presbyterian church, one brightly burning electric cross lighted up the
street. I read dozens and dozens of old American novels and

remembered them every time I passed the old house on Columbia Heights where first Washington Roebling had lived, directing the completion of Brooklyn Bridge from a wheelchair, and
then Hart Crane. I lived with the novels of Rebecca Harding
Davis and Sarah Orne Jewett and William Dean Howells and
Henry James and Hjalmar Boyesen and Henry Blake Fuller,
while Natasha spent fourteen and fifteen hours a day over her
laboratory work and her studies. And I was happy and grateful
for Brooklyn Heights and Brooklyn Bridge and the novels of
William Dean Howells and the Hunt Quartet of Mozart and
the Violin Concerto of Beethoven; on my way home from the
library, passing under our own windows, I would look up to
where I could see Natasha preparing our evening meal, I would
stand in the street just to look up and admire her.

It seemed to me that I was living in the turn of the century I
was beginning to write about, in the dark revolutionary time of
the Eighties and Nineties, with "the struggle for realism" and
the Knights of Labor, and that everything was about to flower
in the revolutionary *avant-garde* of Greenwich Village. When
I read Randolph Bourne and the young Van Wyck Brooks of
America's Coming of Age, I could not feel that 1938 was so far
from 1912. Like so many writers who came of age in the Thirties, I took for granted the continuing spirit of the Twenties
that I knew from *Winesburg, Ohio* and *Prejudices* and *The Sun
Also Rises*. I was sure that we of the revolutionary Thirties
would retain what was vital in the great books of the Twenties
and direct it toward a more hopeful outlook, a fraternal society.
We would improve on the nihilism of Hemingway, the callousness of Mencken, the frivolity of Sinclair Lewis. Like so
many literary radicals who were becoming interested in American literature, I thought I could see across the wasteland of the
Twenties to our real literary brethren in the utopians and Socialist bohemians of 1912. I felt connected to the Socialist

that I loved and everything that I was. I could not believe that Fascism was anything but a temporary aberration; given a fair chance, the people under Nazi rule and Fascist rule would get rid of their oppressors and give themselves to the historical destiny so clearly forseen by liberals and socialists in the nineteenth century. When a classmate of mine just back from the front told me of the massacre by the GPU in Barcelona of Anarchists and anti-Stalinist Communists, I was reluctant to believe him. Although, after years of writing for Cowley at the *New Republic,* I liked him as little as ever and resented his protective benevolence toward "proletarian" literature, which I despised, I shared his feeling that Fascism was the main enemy and I feared any division on the left that might limit maximum resistance to Franco and Hitler. As an influence in literature, the Communists seemed to me idiotic; even Party members now made a point of laughing at the obtuseness of the professional Communist critics. My teaching in the evening session at City College became wearisome as the faithful in my classes resisted every example of free thought, of literary originality. In giving a course on modern fiction, I found to my disgust that half the class refused to read anything by H. G. Wells — he was a "bourgeois liberal." The arrogant stupidity of Communist instructors at this time passed beyond anything I had ever known before. The college *Führer* of the Party was an English instructor with a bad stammer, large spectacles, and a little beard; his middle name was Ulysses, and as he horribly choked out each word in a pronunciamento on the relation of *The Canterbury Tales* to the wool trade in fourteenth-century England, his bearded chin would quiver with agony and his weak frightened eyes would stare up at you while obstinately he ground out the literary law. And one day, when I was offered an editor's job in Washington with the WPA Writers' Project, I went down for my interview in the New York office, somewhere along the waterfront, to enter a room crowded with men and women lying face down on the floor, screaming that they were on strike. In order to get to the supervisor's office at the other end of the hall, I had to make my way over bodies stacked as if after a battle; and as I sat in the supervisor's office, he calmly discussed the job while shouts and screams came from the long hall outside. I made way out again between and over the bodies.

It was the summer of 1939 now. After Hitler's seizure of Czechoslovakia in March, it still seemed to me inconceivable that Russia would not come out against Hitler, and in August, when English and French military missions arrived in Moscow, I took it for granted that some agreement would be made, since of course the Soviet Union wanted peace. On the morning of August 22, I was working happily away at my book and had interrupted myself at noon for a cup of coffee and the news broadcast when it was announced that Ribbentrop was flying to Moscow to sign a non-aggression pact with Stalin the next day, and that the Swastika was already flying over Moscow airport. "No!" I shouted at the radio. "It's not true!" The announcer calmly went on giving the details.

Hitler needed another week to prepare the attack on Poland, but that morning, the Second World War had begun. Stalin had opened the door to war, Stalin had lighted the fuse in Hitler's hand. In everything that the confused American Communists tried to say about the pact, not one seemed to understand that whatever the hesitations of England and France in the past, whatever Russia's own fear of attack, it was wrong to make common cause with Hitler, wrong to expose the world to war. At the signing of the pact, Stalin toasted Hitler's health: "*I know how much the German nation owes to its Führer.*" Every attempt by the creatures of the Communist Party to defend the pact was based on such "realism" and diplomatic "cleverness" — none of these spokesmen for what they called "socialism" seemed to feel anything for the misery of ordinary people in Poland or even Russia. These armchair ideologues of terror and deceit, these bookish exponents of mass murder, these conspiratorial liars talking about historical "justice," now went about explaining how clever Stalin was. They could not get over Stalin's cleverness; it left them simply stupefied with admiration. Yet these same miserable evening college teachers, these pale twenty-five-dollar-a-week accountants, these hysterical claustrophobes of the subway and the tenements, who had lived from day to day in the depression dreaming of the new life that would come to human beings under socialism — these same wretches, who had always assumed their moral superiority to the lords of this earth, now had no sympathy to spare for Warsaw, for the German Communists in Russia who were being delivered by the GPU over the Brest-Litovsk bridge straight into the hands of the Gestapo, for the Polish Jews delivered up to Hitler's proud and masterful murderers, for the French, the English, the Danes, the Norwegians, the Greeks. Russia was saved, and there was not a breath, not a hint, of sympathy for the thousands of human beings who within a week were dead because of Stalin's cleverness. It was "cleverness" they admired — these apostles of brotherhood, these spokesmen for the poor, this "advance guard" of humanity; it was "realism" that now sent them into ecstasies of adoration; even war they loved so long as Russia was spared.

All my life I had lived among people who had seemed to me beautiful because they were the dust of the earth; I had taken literally the claim that they identified their suffering with the liberation of humanity. I now saw that the ideologues among these people had no moral imagination whatever, and no interest in politics. They were merely the slaves of an idea, fetishists of an ideology; the real world did not exist for them, and they would never understand it. They were as cold as their leader, as self-concerned, heartless, mediocre; but being Communists, they existed by an intellectual pretension from which their stupidity would never deliver them. Day after day I followed the *Daily Worker* with savage joy at its confusion as those who had been eloquent about the Okies, the unemployed, the victims of Fascism, now tried to explain the secret contribution that the noble Stalin, the great Stalin, the all-wise and farseeing Stalin, had made to the cause of world peace.

Years later, I heard of a Communist novelist who in September, 1939, had been seized with uncontrollable nervous spasms, and had hauled himself off to the dunes of Provincetown, where he lived alone like an anchorite in the desert, studying Origen and Sir Thomas Browne, and ceaselessly repenting of his "secularism." There were many excellent writers, like Malraux, who in 1939 recognized Soviet self-concern for what it was and went on defending their country against the Nazis and liberty as a universal value. This was true of Malcolm Cowley, Robert Cantwell, Vincent Sheean, Granville Hicks, and most American writers who were not simply political hacks. But in others the Nazi-Soviet pact induced some peculiar changes of heart. As soon as war broke out in September, the State of New York launched an investigation of Communist activity in public schools and colleges, and my old friend Francis, that good "Catholic Socialist," turned himself inside out with fear and repentance. He had been wrong to believe in anything liberal at all, he had betrayed himself and his immortal soul, and as soon as authority tapped him on the shoulder, Francis collapsed, then revived just in time to have discharged from their jobs several people who had been just as disgusted by the Nazi-Communist alliance as he was. After the war, I was to see Francis under many other names. He was the poor boy from the lower East Side who had become Herbert Hoover's most fulsome biographer. He was the "expert on Communism" who sat at the right hand of McCarthy. He was the former editor of a Communist daily in Austria who now lived in Western Germany and preached preventive war against Russia. He was the novelist with the twenty years' nervous illness that kept him from writing anything. He was the "conservative" anthropologist who in the thick of the Negro struggle for civil rights took his position as a "scientist" in favor of racist theories disguised as scholarly criticism. He was the Machiavelli of the managerial revolution who was now advising the advisers to Goldwater. He was the most violent enemy of the New Deal, the most frenzied convert to the Church of England, the most voluble expert on original sin, the man, still, of one idea only. Communism fascinated him more than ever.

Francis was the first holy informer I ever knew; he had been educated first by the Jesuits, then by the Stalinists, and had now gone back to the Jesuits to complete his education. At the end of our college course, at the time of his sudden jump from the mildest liberal heresies to Communism, I had heard nothing from him but ritualistic words about *labor, the working class, surplus value, union of soviet socialist republics, the end of the exploitation of man by man.* Always so meek and mild behind his glasses, with only a faint nervous smile on his lips to indicate the pleasure he took in startling people during his Marxist period, he had often made me think of a priest in mufti. No doubt it had excited him to be a Communist and a Catholic; he had looked humble but sly, like a man who knows that he will yet be in at the death of the old order. But now that Francis had been properly frightened by the ultimate authority — that in charge of education — his double life collapsed, and he was openly hysterical, penitential, "guilty." Everyone was guilty, and in a way everything was, too.

Evil was the prime fact. Man was steeped in it. There is, said Francis to me earnestly, "a Hitler in each of us." With so much guilt at large, there was no need for Francis to worry about anything; he floated in guilt as in a clear mountain spring. I was to observe many veterans of the Thirties in the next years, and mentally divided them between those who had been interested in Communism as a faith and those who had been interested in radical politics. Francis was a saintly informer in the threatening style that was to be the making of Whittaker Chambers: *By these stigmata shall you know me; it is because I am a sinner and the most unworthy of men that you must believe every syllable of what I say about the sickness of the West, which, you must believe me, my children, is* TOTAL.

Francis was in such an ecstasy of self-accusation and re-pentance that he often deliberately invited attacks on himself. I disapproved intensely of the zeal with which he informed on his former comrades, for he was so eager to gain the good opinion of all possible authorities that I suspected him, in his frenzy, of inventing details. But I also felt sorry for him, since he was at such a pitch while the dogmas were fighting each other up and down his soul that I knew that only his religion kept him from committing suicide, and that he was actually inviting murder. He once asked me to lunch with him at a little vegetarian restaurant near the Library where he had often met with his old friends, and as we ate and Francis was berating me for having, in college, started him on the road to perdition by giving him H. G. Wells and Kropotkin to read, I was amazed to find that several people in the restaurant were hissing him. There would have been violence if I had not rushed Francis out of the place, yet there was such a look of righteous injury on his face that I could believe, that afternoon, that the church had found a new martyr.

The new wind shook harder and harder. Hitler crushed Po-

land, and at the end of September, Poland was partitioned between Germany and Russia, as provided by a secret treaty
attached to the Nazi-Soviet "non-aggression pact." Molotov,
who was now Stalin's foreign minister instead of the Jew
Litvinov, explained to the world that "we are coming to the aid
of our blood brothers in the Ukraine." This was the period in
which Molotov spoke of "shortsighted anti-Fascists," and in
which Stalin's telegram to Ribbentrop heralded the Nazi-Soviet
"friendship cemented with blood." Behind the scenes, as we
did not know at the time, the Russians were proceeding to
gather up the Polish intelligentsia and the leaders of the
democratic Socialist movement, so as to liquidate in advance
any possible opposition to a Stalinist Poland after the war.
Behind the scenes, the condemned Jews were being driven
into the ghettoes from which most of them would leave only
to be shot, gassed, starved, hanged, or buried alive.

At the end of November, Russia attacked Finland. I was
sitting one day in the outer office of *Common Sense*, a little
magazine whose writers were united chiefly by idealistic memories of the American Socialist opposition to the First World
War, when a nervous young man with staring eyes came
into the office, went over to the telephone, and calling a newspaper columnist, heatedly denied that the new group of ex-
Communists, of which he was one, were joining the old Communist opposition, Lovestoneite or Trotskyite, that had been
expelled from the Communist Party in the Twenties. He was
in a state of irritable excitement and self-defense very common
in those days, with that slightly orphaned look often seen in
people after a marriage has broken up. He interested me more
than the usual refugees from the Communist Party; he was
bright with social curiosity. Despite his frantic air, he was
actually a skeptical mind, and in the next few years he proved
himself a shrewdly brilliant political reporter. I called him "Ned

Sparks," after the gravel-voiced, testy movie actor of those days who always kept a cigar posted in one corner of his mouth and was untiringly sardonic. With his disheveled hair, a cigarette always burning angrily in his mouth, a seedy raincoat flung over one shoulder, the look of excitedly fighting down his own shyness in order to articulate a thought which, his own skepticism plainly grumbled, would be neither welcomed nor understood, Jim looked like a harried collegian. Yet as I discovered on our walks up and down Columbia Heights, he was peculiarly sensitive to the tragic complexity of the great American books, and he had a comic sense of people's limitations. Unlike so many political refugees in this period, hopelessly drifting from one ideology to another, Jim had come out of his experiences with a vocation for observation and definition. He had become a reporter, and now had a professional but very real detachment, a mocking point of vantage. By devoting himself to the actual organization of society in the United States, he had learned to express our true hopes and fears.

At first I identified him with Granville Hicks and other idealistic radicals of an older generation who had found in Marxism the extension of their Protestant native radicalism. But Jim and Hicks were quite different. Hicks was a moralist in the great American tradition. His Communism had been so pedantic that his pronouncements as literary editor of the *New Masses* had been a burden to the more sophisticated faithful. As a critic, he had seemed to me peculiarly innocent of the experiences described in the rough social documents of the Thirties, but since he was also one of the nicest people in the world, arguing with Hicks made one feel unworthy. There was such a visible honesty and goodness to his person, and he argued so reasonably for anything he believed in, that his position seemed merely one of clear common sense — how

could anyone miss it? He was eminently likable, straightfor-
ward, modest and kind; it was only his predilection for reducing
the most complicated human wants and ideas to his own clear
and shining liberalism that left me at a loss. Ever since the
Nazi-Soviet pact, in a way ever since the Moscow Trials, I had
felt, like the sudden touch of panic, intimations of something
queer, untoward, irreconcilable. There was, definitely, something in the air. Granville had attached himself first to the ideas
of Irving Babbitt, then had preached the social gospel, then
the Socialist and Communist gospel, and after his admirable,
explicit and significant break with the Communists on the basis
of moral principle, was to preach the American small town.
He wrote as if history — even literature — consisted in coher-
ent answers to sensible questions. He was so firmly balanced on
his own magnanimous character and harmonious family life in
the small town where he had settled down that even small towns
now became a social-intellectual principle against the gigantism
and violence of the new age of power upon which America
was entering with the war. "There's only one storm," ran the
old folk saying that gave Hicks the title of his novel of the
period, "and it begins right here."

The approaching storm was to hit some people more than
others.

PART SIX 1940

tween the bay and the ocean, the beach hut where Eugene
O'Neill had spent a season learning to write plays. Nobody I
knew owned a car; people worked till one, when writing broke
up for the day and we all rushed to get on the bus to the
beach; every other day I took first editions of James and
Howells out of the Provincetown Public Library, and in the
mornings worked at a huge old dining table in our cottage,
formerly a stable, that now streamed with the white summer
light that flooded the room from an enormous skylight over
our bed.

I worked at my literary history in such spacious dimensions,
within sight of the white wicker furniture and white fences,
the scrolled fan-shaped armchairs, that I had first seen in the
novels published fifty years earlier. The book that I had begun
against the iron and rusty office buildings left from the Gilded
Age in downtown Brooklyn I was now getting into shape looking over the private lanes that led up to our door in Provincetown; the white picket fences on Priscilla Alden Lane and the
phlox in the garden and the sight of Edmund Wilson carefully
bicycling himself to the Portuguese bakery were also events in
my book, like the Armory Show of 1913 and the friendship of
Randolph Bourne and Van Wyck Brooks. The owner of our
cottage was a swollen and testy old Englishwoman who sat all
day long in the "sun parlor" of her house, which from a rise on
Bradford Street, Provincetown's "back" street, looked over the
bay. There was always a large cane in our landlady's hand, and
whenever I came in on matters concerned with our "studio,"
the sputtering but still despotic force in the old lady's puffy
face and heavily veined hands gave me a moment's glimpse of
a time when people had been larger, bolder. She had a little old
duck of a husband, half her size, who waddled around the place
wearing a yachtsman's cap and carrying a water can; he seemed
always to be watering things; perhaps he hoped to put out the

fires that raged in his wife. Despite the timid little figure he made toddling about with his water can, his voice was so deep and slow that it put you at attention; it had the thickness of soil and made you think of roots and tree bark. He never spoke to his wife without first saluting her as "my dear," yet there was nothing feeble in his gentleness and nothing unpleasant in her power. They were old-fashioned English, cut to a pattern I had never seen before; absolutely without self-consciousness. Their voices resounded with the confident pleasure of their being English. The little man talked with a resounding boom, his wife with a keen, cutting English accent rapidly traversing many successive shades of condescension, personal shyness, unalterable distance from the American tenants and unadmitted interest in them; I was invigorated by personality naturally more positive than anything I had known before.

Our closest friends in Provincetown were a middle-aged radical couple, childless, austere, extraordinarily sweet, among the few survivors of the original idealistic core of the American Communist movement, who had lived in Russia, Spain, Mexico, and had now settled into a small radical sect, really a company of friends, wistfully seeking to stave off American entry into the war.

The Wolfes lived over a wobbly staircase on Commercial Street, in two little rooms, with the same austerity, intellectual faith, the same lovingness toward each other and their trusted friends, that they had shown in Spain, Russia, Mexico. With the little Mexican rugs and pots that they carried with them, the battered suitcases that contained their manuscripts and their favorite books, they looked like the traditionally "pure" couple of radical theory joined by devotion to a common ideal. In their relations with us they were kindly, generous, altogether loving, as in their political thinking they were fiercely separatist from most people in the United States. Natasha and I spent that whole summer under their wing — sitting on the beach together on the gaily striped beach towels that had just come into fashion, on cloudy days walking the Provincetown breakwater from the bay to the ocean, in the evenings sitting on the main pier watching the fishing ships rocking under single lights far out in the harbor. We went off together to the great beaches at Race Point, Long Point, Highland Light in Truro, and plowed together up and down the sand dunes to the Peaked Hills Coast Guard Station to look at shipwrecks and stranded whales. The bleakness of the Cape, the emptiness of those long wild ocean beaches, made me ache with a desire to build something equal to so much empty space. Wildness was still present in the great dunes that began just outside of Provincetown and stretched without interruption from the bay to the ocean. The Wolfes looked after us constantly, guiding us to favorite places and people on the Cape, and the simplicity and earnestness of their lives gave to the modest fish restaurants and open beaches where we spent so much of our time imperishable associations with beach grass, driftwood, an old portable clacking on a kitchen table, fruit juice, espadrilles, and the old-fashioned radical movement. Bert Wolfe had already spent more than ten years eating his heart out at the Communists' betrayal of his movement, and he now went to meals with a medicine bottle containing gastric juice. With his long, lean, bony body in blue trunks, he sat cross-legged on the beach at Provincetown, a volume of the Marx-Engels correspondence in German before him, looking intellectual, saintly and nervous, like a harried American version of Mahatma Gandhi.

It was the summer of 1940; France had already fallen, and the first trickle of a new wave of political refugees was already beginning to appear at the Wolfes', who took in everyone. That summer, Stalin's arm reached to Mexico to put a pickax into the brain of Leon Trotsky; that summer, many a refugee from Hitler and Stalin alike suddenly found that he was barred from Europe, barred from leaving it, and shot himself. Yet listening to the Wolfes and their familiars in the little group on the beach that was by now their wing of their twice-divided political group, I found it possible to believe that we could stay out of the war. We were all Socialists still, and Socialists stayed out of capitalist wars. In 1916 at St. Louis, the American Socialist Party had gone on record against the war, and in 1917 Bert Wolfe and his friends had lost their teaching jobs in the city schools; several had gone to prison. These early experiences had freed him from his routine teaching job to become a professional revolutionary. In 1940, the Second World War invoked in him the same honorable and defiant sense of his duty as a radical. By this time he had lived a dangerous and exhausting life in the Communist opposition to Stalin and had been molded thoroughly by events within the radical movement; his mind was more on Trotsky in 1917 than on Hitler in Paris.

Bert Wolfe was almost the last of his breed, and sitting with him at the end of Provincetown pier, I listened gratefully to his stories of the original Communist International, of John Reed and Angelica Balabanov, Bukharin and Lunacharsky and Trotsky, in those legendary days of the 1920s when the new Communist movement had been led by revolutionary intellectuals. Doctrinaire and fanatical as they had been, they had lived and ruled, they had killed and died, by what they had honestly considered imperatives of the intellect. Stalin did not like intellectuals with that much conviction. Stalin could do something about his jealousies and dislikes. Bert had once heard Stalin, trying to bully members of the American opposition back into line, gleefully boast, case by case, of what he had done to his opponents, rivals and detractors. This had been in the late Twenties, before these same men were brought up in the show trials to accuse themselves of plotting with Hitler against the Soviet state. The victim was usually a revolutionary intellectual of the old type, a "Westerner" who had lived abroad, often a Jew, brought down by the sly and venomous Georgian who, from a rage for unlimited power that could finally be sated only with blood, had killed the theorists, the intellectuals, who still embodied the *élan* of the Russian Revolution. Looking at Bert Wolfe's long thin scholarly frame always ready to leap into discussion, the Bert whom I saw every day with his medicine bottle, his newspaper clippings, his Marxist texts, sitting before a typewriter in his hot little room just under the roof, tapping out fresh polemics in defense of his radical sect, still trying to nail down some disputed point about Soviet history that would bolster his "scientifically" related argument about America's need to stay out of the war, I saw the belief in the "laws" of history that had brought Bert and his friends to become the victims of those who in the name of these "laws" operated as professional sadists, terrorists, inquisitors and policemen. Bert and his wife, who never seemed to speak ill of anyone personally, who had come to value their revolutionary integrity over their very chances of survival, had finally acquired the innocent self-approval which in threadbare clergymen and their wives insulates them against a skeptical world. The very impersonality and loftiness of their principles expressed itself in this refusal to judge persons too closely. Social forces, impersonal as the stars in their courses, made it unnecessary to look sharply at people's personal failings. The Wolfes, by the high-principled kindness with which they accepted us, silently left the implication that any further probing would have been undignified. But when, through them, I met in Provincetown young radical intellectuals and writers of the *Partisan Review* group, notably Mary McCarthy, I noticed the reproach they would never speak, the reproach of their old-fashioned Socialist abstemiousness, against those who had already passed through the radical movement as if it were a bohemian experience.

I met Mary McCarthy through Wolfe, and all the time she spoke to some friends with her fluent style and her nervous laugh, inching her way from personality to personality over boulders of well-chosen words, Wolfe watched her, his mouth open, as if he would never be able to express his amazement. Wolfe and his wife, on principle, avoided personalities; Mary McCarthy dealt in nothing else. She had, I thought, a wholly destructive critical mind, shown in her unerring ability to spot the hidden weakness or inconsistency in any literary effort and every person. To this weakness she instinctively leaped with cries of pleasure — surprised that her victim, as he lay torn and bleeding, did not applaud her perspicacity. She seemed to regard her intelligence as essentially impersonal; truth, in the person of this sharply handsome twenty-eight-year-old Vassar graduate, had come to pass judgment on the damned in Provincetown. Though she was often right enough about the small specific absurdities that she felt compelled to point out about themselves to her friends, she despised the world in which she moved; her judgment represented that insignificant display of cleverness which a cynical society photographer might use in emphasizing a double chin and the dribble from an open mouth.

Mary McCarthy was the first writer of my generation who made me realize that it would now be possible to be a radical without any idealism whatsoever. I was reading Sainte-Beuve that summer in Provincetown, and I was struck by his saying that in France people remain Catholics long after they have ceased to be Christians. Even in conversation, practicing those portraits of familiars who in two years would be expected to recognize themselves in *The Company She Keeps*, she showed that her moving principle was that bleak, unsparing, suspicious view of human nature which is so much admired by reactionaries because it leaves the lower classes so little reason to rebel. Mary was to be stimulated to literary production by the habit of seeing other people as fools. She operated on all her old radical friends, reserving indulgence only for herself. Without the growing conviction of meaninglessness in the air, she might never have felt any authority at all. But bewilderment in the "movement" now set her up exactly as the pathos of the "emancipated" woman of the Twenties had made a world for Dorothy Parker. Among disillusioned radicals, Mary served as governess in the new correctnesses toward which they were moving. She reminded them of the classical learning they had never acquired, the niceties of style they had despised, the social lapses they could no longer overlook. Herself an orphan, with none of the pusillanimous dependence on family love that was the besetting weakness of so many anxious intellectuals, she turned the very outrageousness of her judgments into a social virtue. She operated on her circle, in Provincetown and New York, with open scorn, and impressed them — they who were so solemn — with her power to make them ridiculous. The crispness, hardness, shininess of her performance was the *examen de conscience* to which the sick, deluded ex-utopians, so long victims of their easy credulity, would have to submit. The wretches who had so long believed in revolutionary progress now cowered before the crisp Vassar girl with the Irish jaw who proclaimed the endless treacheries of the human heart — proclaimed it with a discipline of style, a show of classical severity and subtler manners than their own, that pointed up her *right* to take such a very large bite of her victim.

This readiness to total skepticism, to the spirit of comedy,

would have been fruitful in an imaginative dramatist or novelist; but the inner group of *Partisan Review* did not value
imagination. "Who's in it?" I once heard the editor Philip
Rahv ask a writer who submitted a story to him. The *Partisan Review* group were interested in the people around them
to the point of ecstasy; in this world nothing interested them
so much as the personalities of their friends. The ability to ana-
lyze a friend, a trend, a shift in the politico-personal balance of
power, was for them the greatest possible sign of intellectual
power. Creative imagination they unconsciously disdained as
simple-minded — except if it came from the Continent, and
thus could serve as an analogy to their kind of intelligence.
This boundless belief in criticism was actually their passport to
the postwar world, for as society became more complex and
intellectuals more consciously an elite, the old literary radicals
were among the few, in an age of academic criticism, who understood the relation of literature to institutions. Some of these
writers even became the favorite intellectuals of the mass me-
dia, and presiding over the cultural rites of television and the
slicks, delighted their most eager readers by insulting them to
their faces as highbrows, the mass audience, the conformists,
the herd. The intellectuals who had failed at revolution were to
succeed as intellectual arbiters. They had passion. They would
never feel that they had compromised, for they believed in al-
ienation, and would forever try to outdo conventional opinion
even when they agreed with it.

They were intellectuals, and the new age of American
power that was to come with the war was to be more and more
indulgent to intellectuals. But though they were fated to make
brilliant careers in the elitist society that was coming, they
would not be happy. The *élan* of their lives, revolutionary
faith in the future, was missing. ". . . it is possible to be an
atheist, it is possible not to know whether God exists, or why,

and yet believe that man does not live in a state of nature but in history," Nikolai Nikolaievitch, an unfrocked priest, was to say in Pasternak's *Doctor Zhivago*. A Soviet diplomat who committed suicide in 1927 in order to protest Trotsky's expulsion from the Party wrote in his farewell letter: ". . . human life has sense only in so far as it is spent in the service of the infinite — and for us mankind is the infinite. To work for any finite purpose — and everything else is finite — is meaningless. . . . Anything accomplished in our time for mankind's benefit will in some way survive into future ages; and through this our existence acquires the only significance it can possess." History was now a tangle of meanings without clear-cut issue. Meanings there were always plenty of; a critic had only to read a significant book to feel that his inner world was expanding with meaning. But where was the great transformation, which, Marx had promised, would do away with all other faiths? Where was the meaning that had enchanted the poor and intoxicated their visionary and millennial leaders? "There is much suffering in the world," André Malraux one day in New York said in behalf of Spain. "But there is one kind of suffering which it is a privilege to endure, the suffering of those who endure because they want to make a world worthy of man. . . . The life of culture depends less on those who inherit it than on those who desire it. Let each man choose his own way of alleviating this suffering, relieve it he must. That is our responsibility to man's destiny, and perhaps to our own hearts."

Critical intelligence, the old-fashioned kind based on solid moral conceptions, on history as the record of man's progress, was what dominated these ex-radicals; but they no longer identified their ideas with anything but personal strength of mind. They were sour outsiders, analyzing a situation which they could neither join nor control. They were fixed in the habit of intellectual influence, but the influence did not determine the future to which they were dedicated as their own creation. In the years to come, they would shift back and forth amid the ideologies like a fevered patient trying to find a cool place in bed; they would accept any position for a time, no matter how shocking; they would flirt with the most nationalistic and aggressively "realistic" positions. None of these excursions changed them; they would always remain radical intellectuals, dedicated to the better world that only intellectuals had imagined to be possible in practice. After the war, when concrete political issues exploded again, the radical tradition was to become more dynamic than it looked in 1940, in the depths of our defeat. But what would never come back in this most political of ages — not even in Russia — was the faith in a wholly new society that had been implicit in the revolutionary ideal.

There were many ways of taking this. For people like the *Partisan Review* editor Philip Rahv, nothing had happened but that they were out of their natural period, abandoned by their proper *Zeitgeist*. It was impossible to believe that Mary McCarthy had ever been a believing Socialist; she could belong to a radical movement only when it was in decay and objectively ridiculous. Rahv, on the other hand, was an intellectual in the pure Russian style. He would have been happy with Belinsky in 1834, with Chernishevsky in 1861, with Trotsky in 1905; he was not happy with many of his friends after 1936. He was naturally a talker rather than a writer, a pamphleteer, a polemicist, an intellectual master of ceremonies and dominator who just escaped being entirely absorbed in parties, gossip and talk by his genuine absorption in issues and ideas. Even the homely pleasant shreds of Russian accent left over in his speech made him more fascinating as a controversialist than he could ever be as a writer. To listen to Rahv talk with so much passion and scorn, the syllables crunching in his speech with biting Russian sincerity, was to realize that radicalism was Rahv's destiny, his character, his fulfillment. Even when he was most awful in the *Partisan Review* style of personal attack, deliberately outrageous, burying his victim in hot sand up to his neck and smearing his face with honey, you felt that with all the pleasure he took in denouncing wrongdoers, miscreants, bearers of intellectual error, he still looked on people as carriers of ideas, symbols of moral policy, that his fundamental concern was a vision of history and not gossip.

Though Rahv was inherently one of the narrowest men I knew, he was vividly authentic and stimulating as a critic of literature in society. Rahv was so much of a Russian intellectual in the positive, absorbed, evangelical old style, he lived his ideas in conversation; he lived them almost too publicly. I saw him always in a crowd, his impatient, burry accent driving down confused and frivolous people with a force that evoked admiration as well as submission. He was already, in 1940, the Doctor Johnson of his small group of radical intellectuals. In the years to come the social standards of this group became increasingly more sophisticated and demanding, but it did not seem to me that the everlasting atmosphere of the group, the party, the clique, the coterie in which he always moved — that this essential setting had changed at all, or that he functioned at all apart from it. For Rahv a piece of writing was not real unless it appeared in the immediate social setting of a magazine and evoked an immediate social response in conversation, rebuttal, polemic. Literature for him came out of social tension, and to social tension it had to contribute; literature was the product of social debate — and Rahv's ideal aim was to add to it. This could be overdone, and there was much in Rahv's circle, where people seemed to sit for a long evening glued to each other in fascination with the weaknesses that could be turned to immediate account, that was cruel but comic. This *avant-garde* gnawed on each other, lived on each other. Yet though the very basis of the association that *Partisan Review* editors and writers had with each other was a kind of group identification, these people saw themselves as loyal to a great cultural tradition. It was my tradition. We shared a fundamental realism about our society and obstinate hopes for mankind that were to be conspicuously missing from the intellectual scene as America went to war again.

EPILOGUE 1945

ONE DAY IN the fall of 1940, when the United States had begun to rearm on a great scale, I sat in a newsreel theater on Broadway looking at lines of tanks and heavy guns lumbering heavily, busily, cheerfully out of the factories like new automobiles, and knew that the depression was over. The depression ended only with the war, and the war created a new age of unique and boundless technical power that was to make the lean and angry Thirties seem the end of the old dog-eat-dog society and not the beginning of a new.

It was the war that launched us on our present confidence

and power — and the war, in the form of permanent rearma-
ment, goes on and on, incidentally protecting us from another
period of mass unemployment and social hysteria. Probably
nothing so disruptive of the social order will again be allowed
to spread. The war was the first payment on the more accomplished society in which we are now living. It was a sacrifice to
progress.

One day in the spring of 1945, when the war against Hitler
was almost won, I sat in a newsreel theater in Piccadilly looking at the first films of newly liberated Belsen. On the screen,
sticks in black-and-white prison garb leaned on a wire, staring
dreamily at the camera; other sticks shuffled about, or sat
vaguely on the ground, next to an enormous pile of bodies,
piled up like cordwood, from which protruded legs, arms,
heads. A few guards were collected sullenly in a corner, and
for a moment a British Army bulldozer was shown digging an
enormous hole in the ground. Then the sticks would come
back on the screen, hanging on the wire, looking at us.

It was unbearable. People coughed in embarrassment, and in
embarrassment many laughed.